Freemasonry &
Catholicism

By Max Heindel

Copyright © 2021 Lamp of Trismegistus. All rights reserved. No part of this publication may be reproduced or transmitted in any form or by any means, electronic or mechanical, including photocopying, recording, or by any information storage and retrieval system, without permission in writing from Lamp of Trismegistus. Reviewers may quote brief passages.

ISBN: 978-1-63118-508-3

*Foundations of Freemasonry
Series*

Other Books in this Series and Related Titles

Masonic and Rosicrucian History by M P Hall & H Voorhis (978-1-63118-486-4)

The Kabbalah of Masonry & Related Writings by E Levi &c (978-1-63118-453-6)

Some Deeper Aspects of Masonic Symbolism by A E Waite (978-1-63118-461-1)

Masonic Symbolism of King Solomon's Temple by A Mackey &c (978-1-63118-442-0)

The Old Past Master by Carl H Claudy (978-1-63118-464-2)

The Influence of Pythagoras on Freemasonry and Other Essays (978-1-63118-404-8)

The Mysteries of Freemasonry & the Druids by various (978-1-63118-444-4)

Rosicrucians and Speculative Masonry in the Seventeenth Century (978-1-63118-489-5)

The Two Great Pillars of Boaz and Jachin by A Mackey &c (978-1-63118-433-8)

The Regius Poem or Halliwell Manuscript by King Solomon (978-1-63118-447-5)

The Lost Keys of Freemasonry or The Secret of Hiram Abiff (978-1-63118-427-7)

The Master Mason's Handbook by J S M Ward (978-1-63118-474-1)

Brothers & Builders by Joseph Fort Newton (978-1-63118-506-9)

Symbolism and Discourses on the Entered Apprentice, Fellowcraft and Master Mason Blue Lodge Degrees by various (978-1-63118-413-0)

Freemasonry in the Medieval or Middle Ages by various (978-1-63118-450-5)

American Indian Freemasonry by A C Parker (978-1-63118-460-4)

Freemasonry, Mithraism and the Ancient Mysteries by various (978-1-63118-407-9)

The Ceremony of Initiation: Analysis & Commentary (978-1-63118-473-4)

The Symbols and Legends of Masonry by C H Vail (978-1-63118-504-5)

The Janeites, The Man Who Would Be King and Other Stories of Freemasonry by Rudyard Kipling (978-1-63118-480-2)

Audio Versions are also available on Audible, Amazon and Apple

Other Books in this Series and Related Titles

Rosicrucian Rules, Secret Signs, Codes and Symbols by various (978-1-63118-488-8)

History and Teachings of the Rosicrucians by W W Westcott &c (978-1-63118-487-1)

The Rosicrucian Chemical Marriage by Christian Rosenkreuz (978-1-63118-458-1)

The Rosicrucian Fama Fraternitatis and Confessio Fraternitatis (978-1-63118-454-3)

Freemasonry and the Egyptian Mysteries by C. W. Leadbeater (978-1-63118-456-7)

Qabbalistic Teachings and the Tree of Life by M P Hall (978-1-63118-482-6)

The Sepher Yetzirah and the Qabalah by M P Hall (978-1-63118-481-9)

Cloud Upon the Sanctuary by K. Eckartshausen (978-1-63118-438-3)

An Outline of Theosophy by C. W. Leadbeater (978-1-63118-452-9)

The Psalms of Solomon by King Solomon (978-1-63118-439-0)

Masonic Symbolism of the Apron & the Altar by various (978-1-63118-428-4)

The Book of Wisdom of Solomon by King Solomon (978-1-63118-502-1)

Masonic Symbolism of Easter and the Christ in Masonry (978-1-63118-434-5)

The Odes of Solomon by King Solomon (978-1-63118-503-8)

Ancient Mysteries and Secret Societies by M P Hall (978-1-63118-410-9)

The Golden Verses of Pythagoras: Five Translations (978-1-63118-479-6)

A Few Masonic Sermons by A. C. Ward &c (978-1-63118-435-2)

Lost Chapters of the Book of Daniel and Related Writings (978-1-63118-417-8)

Arcane Formulas or Mental Alchemy by W W Atkinson (978-1-63118-459-8)

The Legend of the Holy Grail and its Connection with Templars and Freemasons by A E Waite (978-1-63118-462-8)

The Leadbeater Reader: A Selection of Occult Essays (978-1-63118-483-3)

Audio versions are also available on Audible, Amazon and Apple

Table of Contents

Introduction...7

Freemasonry & Catholicism

Part I: *Lucifer, the Rebel Angel*...9

Part II: *The Masonic Legend*...16

Part III: *The Queen of Sheba*...23

Part IV: *Casting the Molten Sea*...32

Part V: *The Mystery of Melchisedec*...37

Part VI: *Spiritual Alchemy*...49

Part VII: *The Philosopher's Stone: What it is and How it is Made*...56

Part VIII: *The Path of Initiation*...66

Part IX: *Armageddon, the Great War and the Coming Age*...72

Summary...77

INTRODUCTION

From the beginning of Modern Freemasonry's birthdate of 1717, the intelligentsia of humanity have found refuge for safe reflection within the walls of the fraternity. Masonic writers have produced a nearly incalculable amount of written musings on a multitude of esoteric and philosophical subjects, as they relate to the ancient mysteries that Freemasonry currently storehouses. Sadly, most of it appears to have sat largely unread, as American Freemasonry in particular, continues to transform itself into something that bears little resemblance to what it was originally designed to be. The true essence of Freemasonry is not that of blind patriotism or a single-minded national religion but one of Universal Brotherhood and altruism, designed for the betterment not just of its members but of society as a whole. In particular, for those who are not members of the fraternity, as Freemasonry has always acted as a beacon, to help guide humanity through darker times, with the hopes that one day we will collectively reach a truly enlightened age.

It's not uncommon for new members joining the fraternity to find little education within the walls of many modern lodges, in spite of so much written material available to the membership. Many older members are not simply uneducated with regards to real Masonic history and symbology, not to mention the vast arena of related subjects, but they are disinterested in all of it, as well.

Lamp of Trismegistus is doing its part to help preserve humanity's Masonic history by making some of these classics available to those students who are seeking to unearth the knowledge of these ancient colossi. As such, Lamp of Trismegistus offers its readers highlights of Masonic study, culled from a variety of authors and viewpoints, with the hope bringing education back into the fraternity. So, be sure to check out other titles in our *Foundations of Freemasonry Series* as well as our *Theosophical Classics, Occult Fiction, Paranormal Research Series, Esoteric Classics, Supernatural Fiction, Studies in Buddhism* and our *Christian Apocrypha Series* as well as numerous other subjects; and, don't be afraid to let a little altruism into your own heart or even into your Lodge. You can also download the audio versions of many of these titles from Audible, Amazon or Apple, for learning on the go.

PART I
LUCIFER, THE REBEL ANGEL

The Rosicrucian Fellowship aims to educate and construct, to be charitable even to those from whom we differ, and never to vent the venom of vituperation, spite, or malice even upon those who seem deliberately determined to mislead. We revere the Catholic religion; it is as divine in its essence, as both were born to further the aspiration of the striving soul, and both have a message and a mission in the world not apparent upon the surface today, because man-made ceremonial as a scale has hidden the present articles to remove that scale and show the Cosmic purpose of these two Great Organizations, which are so bitterly antagonistic to each other. We do not aim to reconcile them, however, for though they are both designed to further the emancipation of the soul, their methods are different, and the attributes of the soul fostered by one method will indeed be very different from the quality of the soul nurtured in the other School. Therefore, the strife must continue until the battle for the souls of men has been lost and won. The issue is not, however, the persistence of the Masonic or Catholic institutions; but the outcome will determine the nature of the training humanity will receive in the remaining Periods of our evolution. We shall endeavor to show the cosmic root of both of these institutions, the purpose of each and the training which each will inaugurate, if successful; also the nature of the soul quality which may be expected to result from each method.

Our opposition is not fanatical, or blind to the merits of the Catholic Religion, however. The Catholic is our brother as well as the Mason; we would not say a disparaging, irreverent word against this faith, or those who live by it, and should we seem to do so, in any passage, the wrong will be due to inadvertence. The reader is requested to note that we distinguish sharply between the Catholic

Hierarchy and the Catholic Religion, but the former are also our brothers; we would not throw stones either physically or morally, for we know our own shortcomings too well to attack others. Thus our opposition is not personal, but spiritual, and to be fought with the weapon of the Spirit--Reason. We firmly believe it to be for the everlasting good of mankind that the Masons should win, and cannot therefore be sure to present the Catholic side in a perfectly unbiased manner, but we ask our students for whom this is written, to believe that we shall try to be just. Of the Cosmic Facts we are certain, but bias may creep into our conclusions, therefore each must use his reason to test what we have to say, viz., "prove all things and hold fast that which is good."

The great law of analogy is everywhere the master key of all spiritual mysteries, and, although Masonry and Catholicism do not begin till we arrive at the Earth Period, they have their prototype in the earlier Periods; we shall therefore briefly touch upon the essential facts.

In the Saturn Period, the Earth-in-the-making was dark; HEAT, which is the manifestation of the ever invisible fire, was the only element then manifest; embryonic mankind was mineral like, the only lower kingdom of evolving life. Unity was everywhere observable, and the Lords of Mind who were human then, were at one among themselves.

In the Western Wisdom Teaching we speak of the highest Initiate of the Saturn Period as THE FATHER.

In the Sun Period the root of a new element, AIR, was evolved, and coalesced with the true fire, which, mark again, is always invisible, and which manifested as HEAT in the Saturn Period. Then fire burst into FLAMES, and the dark world became a blazing ball of luminous fire-mist at the word of power, "LET THERE BE LIGHT."

Let the student ponder well the relation of FIRE and FLAME; the former lies sleeping, invisible in everything, and is kindled into light in various ways: by a blow of a hammer upon a stone, by friction of wood against wood and by chemical action, etc. This gives us a clue to the identity and state of THE FATHER, "whom no man hath seen at any time" but who is revealed in "The Light of the World," the Son, who is the highest Initiate of the Sun Period. As the unseen fire is revealed in the flame, so also the fullness of the Father dwelt in the Son, and they are one as fire is one with the flame in which it manifests. This is the root of all true Sun and Fire worship. All look beyond the physical symbol and adore "Our Father Who art in Heaven." The Mystic Masons of today hold this faith in fire as firmly as ever.

Thus it will be seen that the Unity which prevailed in the Saturn Period continued in the Sun Period. The ordinary humanity of that time has now evolved to the glory of Archangels; some were more advanced than others, but there was no antagonism among them. Our present humanity had advanced to a plantlike stage, and was slightly above the new Lifewave started in the Sun Period, and unity also here prevailed.

In the Moon Period contact of the heated sphere with cold Space generated moisture, and the battle of the elements commenced in all its fierceness. The heated ball of fire endeavored to evaporate the moisture, force it outwards and create a vacuum wherein to maintain its integrity and burn undisturbed; but there is and can be no void in nature, hence the outrushing steam condensed at a certain distance from the heated ball and was again driven inwards by the cold of Space, to be again evaporated and propelled outwards, in a ceaseless round forages and ages, as a shuttlecock between the separate Hierarchies of Spirits composing the various Kingdoms of Life, represented in the Fire-Sphere and Cosmic Space which is an expression of the Homogeneous Absolute Spirit. The

Fire Spirits are actively striving to attain enlargement of consciousness. But the Absolute rests ever clothed in the invisible garment of Cosmic Space. In 'It' all powers and possibilities are LATENT, and It seeks to discourage and check any attempt at expenditure of latent power as dynamic energy required in the evolution of a solar system. Water is the agent It used to quench the fire of active spirits. The zone between the heated center of the separate Spirit Sphere, and the Point where its individual atmosphere meets Cosmic Space, is a battleground of evolving spirits at various stages of evolution.

The present Angels were human in the Moon Period, and the highest Initiate is The Holy Spirit, (Jehovah).

As our humanity and the other Kingdoms of Life on earth are variously affected by the present elements, so that some like heat, others prefer cold, some thrive on moisture and others require dryness, so also in the Moon Period among the Angels, some had affinity for water, others abhorred it and loved fire.

The continued cycles of condensation and evaporation of the moisture surrounding the fiery center eventually caused incrustation, and it was the purpose of Jehovah to mold this "red earth," translated ADAM, into forms wherein to imprison and QUENCH THE SPIRITS OF THE FIRE. To this end, He issued the creative fiat, and the prototypes of fish, fowl and every living thing appeared, even including the primitive human form, which were created by His Angels; thus He hoped to make all that lives and moves subservient to His will. Against this plan a minority of the Angels rebelled; they had too great an affinity for FIRE to bear contact with water, and refused to create the forms as ordered; but thereby they at the same time deprived themselves of an opportunity of evolution along the conventional lines, and became an anomaly in nature; furthermore, having repudiated the authority of Jehovah, they must work out their own salvation in their own manner. How this has been accomplished by LUCIFER, their Great Leader will be made plain in the following articles; for the present, suffice it to say, that in the Earth Period, when various planets were differentiated to provide proper evolutionary environment for each class of Spirits, the Angels under Jehovah were set to work with the inhabitants of ALL PLANETS HAVING MOONS; while the Lucifer Spirits have their abode upon the planet Mars. The Angel GABRIEL is representative on earth, of the Lunar Hierarchy, presided over by Jehovah; the Angel SAMAEL is ambassador of the Martial forces of Lucifer. Gabriel (who announced the coming birth of Jesus to Mary) and his lunar angels are therefore the givers of physical life, while Samael and the hosts of Mars are the Angels of Death.

Thus originated the feud in the dim dawn of this Cosmic day, and that which we see as Free Masonry today is an attempt by the HIERARCHS OF FIRE, the Lucifer Spirits, to bring us the imprisoned spirit 'LIGHT,' that by it we may SEE and KNOW. Catholicism is an activity of the HIERARCHS OF WATER, and places 'HOLY WATER' at the Temple door to quench the spirits seeking light and knowledge and to inculcate FAITH in Jehovah.

As the vernal equinox is said to be at the first point of Aries, no matter where in the constellations it falls by precession, so the point where the human seed-atom comes from the invisible world and is taken in hand by the Lunar God of Generation, Jehovah, through his ambassador, the Angel Gabriel, is esoterically the first point of Cancer. This is the Cardinal sign of the watery Triplicity, and is ruled by the Moon. There Conception takes place; but were the form built of water and its concretions alone, it could never come to birth, so four months later when the fetus has reached the stage of development corresponding to the second sign of the watery triplicity, Scorpio, the eighth sign, which corresponds to the house of death, Samael, the dauntless ambassador of the Lucifer Spirits, invades the watery domain of the Lunar Hierarchy and introduces the fiery spark of the spirit into the inert form, to leaven, quicken and mould it into an expression of itself.

There the Silver Cord which has grown from the seed-atom of the dense body (located in the heart) since conception, is welded to the part that has sprouted from the central vortex of the desire body, (located in the liver) and when the Silver Cord is tied by the seed-atom of the vital body, (located in the solar plexus) the spirit DIES to life in the super-sensible world, and quickens the body it is to use in its coming earth life. This life on earth last until the course of events foreshadowed in the wheel of life, the horoscope, has been run; and when the spirit again reaches the realm of Samael, the Angel of Death, the mystic eighth house, the silver cord is loosed, and the spirit returns to God who gave it, until the dawn of another Life-day in the School of earth beckons it to a new birth that it may acquire more skill in the arts and crafts of temple-building.

About five months after the quickening, when the last of the watery signs, Pisces, has been passed, the representative of the Lucifer Spirits, Samael, focuses the forces of the fiery sign, Aries, where Mars is positively polarized, so that under the impulse of their dynamic energy the waters of the womb are voided, and the imprisoned spirit is liberated into the physical world, to fight the battle of life. It may blindly butt its head against the Cosmic forces typified by the first of the fiery signs, Aries, the Ram, which is a symbol of the brute strength brought to bear upon the problems of life by the most primitive races; or it may adopt the more modern method of cunning, as a means of attaining mastery over others, which characteristic is indicated in the second of the fiery signs, Leo, the Lion, the king of beasts; or perchance it may rise above the animal nature, and aim at the stars with the bow of spiritual aspiration, typified by the last of the fiery signs, Sagittarius, the Centaur. The Centaur is just ahead of the watery sign Scorpio, a warning that one who tries to reach that prerogative as "PHREE

MESSEN," a son of Fire and Light, will surely feel the sting of the Scorpion in his heel, which will goad him onward upon the path where men become "wise as serpents." It is from this class that Mystic Masonry is recruited with men who have the indomitable courage TO DARE, the unflagging energy TO DO and the diplomatic discrimination TO BE SILENT.

PART II
THE MASONIC LEGEND

Every mystic movement has its legend, which tells in symbolic language its status in the cosmic order and the ideal which it tries to realize. From the Old Testament, containing the Atlantean Mystery teaching, we learn that mankind was created male-female, bisexual, and that each one was capable of propagating his species without the cooperation of another as is the case with some plants today. Later on, we are informed, Jehovah removed one pole of the creative force from ADAM, the early humanity, and that there were henceforth two sexes. The esoteric teaching supplements this information by stating that the purpose of this change was to use one pole of the creative force for the building of a brain and larynx wherewith mankind might acquire knowledge and express itself in speech. The intimate connection between the organs, brain, larynx and genitals is evident to anyone upon the slightest examination of facts. The boy's voice changing at puberty, the mental deficiency resulting from overindulgence of the passional nature, and the inarticulate speech of the mentally facts which might be added prove this assertion.

According to the Bible, our earliest parents were forbidden to eat of THE TREE OF KNOWLEDGE, but Eve, seduced by the serpent, did eat and later induced the man to follow her example. Who the serpents are and what the Tree of Knowledge is may also be determined from certain passages in the Bible. We are told, for instance, that Christ exhorted his disciples to be "wise as serpents and harmless as doves." The so-called curse pronounced upon Eve after her confession declares that she must bear her children in sorrow and pain and that the race will die. It has always been a great stumbling block to Bible commentators as to what connection there could be between the eating of an apple, death, and painful parturition; but when we are acquainted with the chaste expressions of the Bible, which designates the creative act by such passages as "Adam KNEW Eve and she bore Abel," "How can I bear a child seeing I KNOW not a man?" et cetera, it is very evident that the Tree of Knowledge is a symbolical expression for the creative act. Then it is plain that the serpents taught Eve how to perform the creative act and that Eve instructed Adam. Therefore, Christ designated the serpents as harmful while admitting their wisdom. To get at the identity of the serpent it is necessary to invoke the esoteric teaching, which points them out as the martial Lucifer Spirits, rulers of the serpentine sign Scorpio. Their Initiates, even so late as the Egyptian Dynasty, wore the URAEUS or serpent symbol in the forehead as a sign of the source of their wisdom.

As a consequence of this unauthorized use of the creative force, humanity ceased to be ethereal and crystallized into the COATS OF SKIN or physical body which now hides from them the gods who dwell in the invisible realms; and great was their sorrow at this loss.

GENERATION had been originally established by the Angels under Jehovah. It was then performed in great temples under propitious planetary conditions and parturition was then painless, as it is today among wild animals where the creative function is not abused for the purpose of gratifying the senses.

DEGENERATION resulted from the ignorant and unauthorized abuse inaugurated by the Lucifer Spirits.

REGENERATION must be undertaken in order to restore man to his lost estate as a spiritual being and to free him from this body of death wherein he is now encrusted. Death must be swallowed up in Immortality.

To attain this object, a covenant was made with humanity when it was expelled from the garden of God to wander in the wilderness of the world. According to that plan, a Tabernacle was built after a pattern planned by God, Jehovah, and an ark symbolical of the human spirit was placed in it. Its staves were never taken out of their place, to show that man is a pilgrim on the earth and may never rest until he reaches the goal. There was within it a golden pot with "MANNA" (man) "FALLEN FROM HEAVEN," together with a statement of the divine laws which man must learn in his pilgrimage through the wilderness of matter. This symbolic ark contained also a magic wand, an emblem of the spiritual powers, called AARON'S ROD, which are now latent in everyone on his way to the haven of rest--the mystic temple of Solomon. The Old Testament also tells how humanity was miraculously led and provided for, how after the warfare with the world it was given peace and prosperity by the before mentioned King Solomon; in short, stripped of all embellishments the story relates the salient facts of man's descent from heaven, his principal metamorphoses, his transgression of the laws of the God Jehovah would wish to guide him in the future till he reaches the Kingdom of Heaven- -the land of peace--and again docilely follows the lead of the Divine Ruler.

THE MASONIC LEGEND has points of variance from as well as agreement with the Bible story. It states that Jehovah created EVE, that the Lucifer Spirit SAMAEL united with her but that he was ousted by Jehovah and forced to leave her before the birth of her son Cain, who was thus THE SON Of A WIDOW. Then Jehovah created ADAM, to be the husband of Eve, and from their union Abel was born. Thus from the beginning there have been two kinds of people in the world. One begotten by the Lucifer Spirit Samael and partaking of a semi-divine nature imbued with the dynamic martial energy inherited from this divine ancestry, is aggressive, progressive, and possessed of great initiative, but impatient of restraint or authority whether human or divine. This class is loath to take things on faith and prone to prove all things by the light of reason. These people BELIEVE IN WORKS rather than faith, and by their dauntless courage and inexhaustible energy they have transformed the trackless wilderness of the world to a garden full of life and beauty, so lovely in fact that THE SONS OF CAIN have forgotten the garden of God, the Kingdom of Heaven, whence they were expelled by the decree of the lunar God Jehovah. Against Him they are in constant rebellion because He has tied them by THE UMBILICAL "CABLE TOW." They have lost their spiritual sight and are imprisoned in the forehead of the body where it is said Cain was marked; they must wander as prodigal sons in the comparative darkness of the material world, oblivious to their high and noble estate until they find the door of the temple, and ask and receive LIGHT; then as "PHREE MESSEN" or children of light they are instructed in methods of building a new temple without sound of hammer, and when the spirit realizes that it is far from its heavenly home, a prodigal, feeding upon the unsatisfactory husks of the material world, that apart from the Father it is "POOR, NAKED AND BLIND," when it knocks at the door of a mystic temple like that of the Rosicrucians and asks for light, when it receives the desired instruction after due qualification by building and ethereal soul-body, a temple or house eternal in the heavens, not made with hands, and without sound of hammer, when its nakedness is clothed with that house (see Cor. 4.5,) then the neophyte receives "THE WORD," the open sesame to the inner worlds and learns to travel in foreign parts in the invisible worlds. There he takes soul-flights into heavenly regions and qualifies for higher degrees under more direct instruction from THE GRAND ARCHITECT OF THE UNIVERSE, who fashioned both heaven and earth.

Such is the temperament of THE WIDOW'S SONS inherited from their divine progenitor Samael and given by him to their ancestor Cain. Their past history is a struggle with adverse conditions, their achievement is victory wrested from all opposing forces by indomitable courage and persistent effort, unchecked by temporary defeat.

On the other hand while Cain, governed by divine ambition, toiled and tilled the soil to make two blades of grass grow where there was only one, ABEL, THE HUMAN PROGENY OF HUMAN PARENTS, felt no urge or unrest, himself a creature of Jehovah through Adam and Eve; he was perfectly contented to tend the flocks also created by God and to accept a livelihood from their divinely begotten increase without labor or exercising initiative. This docile attitude was most pleasing to the God Jehovah, who was extremely jealous of His prerogative as Creator. Therefore He cordially accepted the offering of Abel obtained without effort or initiative, but scorned the offering of Cain because derived through his own divine creative instinct akin to that of Jehovah. Cain then slew Abel, but did not thereby exterminate the docile creatures of Jehovah, for we are told ADAM KNEW EVE AGAIN AND SHE BORE SETH. Seth had the same characteristics as Abel and transmitted them to his descendants, who to this day, continue to trust to the Lord for everything, and WHO LIVE BY FAITH AND NOT BY WORK. By arduous and energetic application to the world's work the Sons of Cain have acquired worldly wisdom and temporal power. They have been captains of industry and masters of STATECRAFT, while the Sons of Seth, looking to the Lord for guidance, have become the avenue for divine and spiritual wisdom. They constitute the PRIESTCRAFT. The animosity of Cain and Abel has been perpetuated from generation to generation among their respective descendants. Nor could it be otherwise, because one class as temporal rulers aim to lift humanity to physical well-being through conquest of the material world, while the Priesthood is their role as spiritual guides urge their followers to forsake the wicked world, the vale of tears, and look to God for comfort. One school aims to turn out MASTER workmen, skilled in the use of tools wherewith they may wrest a livelihood from the earth, which was cursed by their divine adversary Jehovah. The other produces MASTER MAGICIANS, skilled in the use of the tongue in invocation, and by the use of the tongue they gain support from the toilers here and pray themselves and their charges into heaven hereafter.

After the future in store for the Sons of Cain and their followers, the temple legend is also most eloquent. It states that from Cain descended Methuselah, who invented writing, Tubal Cain, a cunning worker in metals, and Jubal, who originated music. In short, THE SONS OF CAIN ARE THE ORIGINATORS OF THE ARTS AND CRAFTS. Therefore when Jehovah chose Solomon, the scion of the race of Seth, to build a house for his name, the sublime spirituality of a long line of divinely guided ancestors flowered into the conception of the magnificent temple called Solomon's Temple, though Solomon has only the instrument to carry out the divine plan revealed by Jehovah to David. But Solomon was unable to execute the divine design in concrete form. Therefore it became necessary for him to apply to King Hiram of Tyre, the descendent of Cain, who selected HIRAM ABIFF, THE SON OF A WIDOW, (as all Free Masons are called because of the relation of their divine progenitor with Eve.) Hiram Abiff then became Grand Master of the army of construction. In him the arts and crafts of all the Sons of Cain who had gone before had flowered. He was skilled beyond all others in the work of the world, without which the plan of Jehovah must have remained forever a divine dream, and could never have become a concrete reality. The worldly acumen of the Sons of Cain was as necessary to the completion of this temple as the spiritual conception of the Sons of Seth, and, therefore, during the period of construction the two classes joined forces, the underlying enmity being hidden under a superficial show of amity. It was, indeed, the first attempt to unite them, and had that been accomplished the world history from then on would have been altered in a very material manner.

The Sons of Cain, descended from the fiery Lucifer Spirits, were naturally proficient in the use of FIRE. By it the metals hoarded by Solomon and his ancestors were melted into altars, lavers and vessels of various kinds. Pillars were fashioned by workmen under the direction of Hiram Abiff, and arches to rest upon them. The great edifice was nearing completion when he made ready to cast the "molten sea," which was to be the crowning effort, his masterpiece. It was in the construction of this great work that the treachery of the Sons of Seth became manifest and frustrated the divine plan of reconciliation. They tried to quench the fire used by Hiram Abiff with their natural weapon, WATER, and almost succeeded. The incidents which led up to this catastrophe, their meaning, and the sequel will be related in the next chapter.

PART III
THE QUEEN OF SHEBA

The Masonic Legend is voluminous, circumstantial, even trivial, and seemingly farfetched and fantastic to the uninitiated who fail to see the important hidden meaning underlying every word; but we will give only such fragments as have a bearing upon our main subject and the explanation necessary to link them together.

The events which led up to the conspiracy again our last chapter, and which culminated in his murder, commenced with the arrival of the Queen of Sheba who had been attracted to the court of Solomon by tales of his wonderful wisdom and of the splendor of the temple he was engaged in building. She is said to have come laden with gorgeous gifts and it is stated that at first she was much impressed with the wisdom of Solomon. But even the Bible, which is written from the standpoint of the Jehovistic Hierarchies, hints that she saw at the court of Solomon one that was fairer than he, and there the Bible narrative leaves her. Her marriage with Solomon was never consummated or the name of Mason would have faded from memory long ere the present day and humanity at large would now be docile children of the dominant church, without free will, choice or prerogative. Nor could she be permitted to wed Hiram, who represented the temporal power, or Religion would have been stamped out; she must wait for the bridegroom who shall embody within himself the combined good qualities of Solomon and Hiram, but who is purified from their weaknesses. For the Queen of Sheba is the COMPOSITE SOUL OF HUMANITY, and at the consummation of the work of our evolutionary era she will be the bride, while Christ, whom Paul called a High Priest after the order of Melchisedec, will fill the dual office of both spiritual and temporal head, where He will be both king and priest, to the eternal welfare of mankind at large who are now in bondage either to church or state but waiting, whether they realize it or not, for the day of emancipation, symbolically represented as the Millennium, when there will be a wonderful city, a new Jerusalem, A CITY OF PEACE. And the earlier this amalgamation can be brought about, the better for humanity. Therefore, an attempt was made at the time and is the place which is said in the Legend to be the scene of Solomon's and Hiram's love episode. There the two Initiatory Orders met for the consummation of a definite work of amalgamation symbolically called THE MOLTEN SEA, a work which was then attempted for the first time. It could not have been wrought at any earlier period, for man was not sufficiently advanced. At that time, however, it seemed as if the united efforts of the two schools might accomplish the task, and had it not been for the desire of each to oust the other from the affections of the symbolic Queen of Sheba, the soul of humanity, they might have succeeded, an equitable union between Church and State might have been effected and human evolution might have been greatly furthered. But both Church and State were jealous of their particular prerogative; the Church would only amalgamate upon condition that she retain all her ancient power over mankind, and take in addition those of the temporal government. The State was selfish in a similar manner and the Queen of Sheba, humanity at large, is still unwed. The Masonic Legend tells the story of the attempt and its failure as follows:

When the Queen of Sheba had been shown the gorgeous palace of Solomon and had bestowed her choice gifts of gold and wrought work, she asked also to be shown the great Temple which was nearing completion. She marveled much at the magnitude of the work but wondered at the seeming absence of workmen, and the stillness about the place. And she therefore requested Solomon to call the workmen that she might see who had wrought this wonder; but though the servants of Solomon at the palace obeyed the slightest wish of the monarch, and although he had been appointed by the God Jehovah to build the temple, these workmen were not subject to his authority; they only yielded obedience to one who had "THE WORD" and "THE SIGN." Therefore no one appeared at the call of Solomon, and the Queen of Sheba could not escape the conclusion that this marvelous miracle was wrought by another and one who was greater than Solomon. And so she insisted on knowing and seeing this KING OF CRAFTS and his wonderful workmen, much to the chagrin of Solomon, who felt that he had fallen in her estimation.

The temple of Solomon is our Solar Universe which forms the great school of life for our evolving humanity; the broad lines of its history, past, present and future, are written in the stars, its main outlines being discernible to anyone of average intelligence. In the Microcosmic scheme, the temple of Solomon is also the body of man wherein the individualized spirit or ego is evolving, as God is in the great universe. Work on the true temple, as we are told in 2nd Corinthians, fifth chapter, is wrought by invisible forces working in silence, building the temple without sound of hammer. As the temple of Solomon was visible in all its glory to the Queen of Sheba, so the evidence of the toil of these invisible forces is easily perceived, both in the universe and in man, but they themselves keep in the background and work without ostentation; they hide from all who have not the right to see them or to command them. The relation of these nature forces to the work they do in the universe may perhaps be better understood when we use an illustration: Let us suppose that a carpenter wishes to build a house wherein to live. He selects a place whereon to build and brings the materials thither, then with the tools of his trade he commences to lay the foundation. Gradually the walls are put up, the roof put on, the inside completed and the structure finished. During all the time while he is working, a dog, which is an intelligent spirit belonging to another and later life-wave of evolution, watches his actions and the whole process of construction and sees the house gradually take shape and reach completion. But it lacks the proper understanding of what he is doing and of what is the ultimate purpose in his mind. Let us now suppose that the dog were unable to see the carpenter or to hear the noise made by his hammer and other tools. Then it would be in the same relation to this builder, as humanity at large is to the Architect of the Universe and the forces which work under His command. For the dog would then see only the materials coming together slowly and taking shape, finally forming a finished structure. Humanity also sees the silent growth of plant, of beast and of bird, but is unable to understand what causes this physical growth and the changes in the visible universe, for it does not see the immense army of invisible workmen who are silently toiling in the soundless silence to bring about these results. Nor do they respond to the call of anyone who has not the sign and the word of power, no matter how high his standing or station in the world.

The Churchman always emphasizes the necessity of faith, while the Statesman emphasizes, and places his reliance on, WORK. But when faith flowers into work we reach the highest ideal of expression. Humanity may, and does, admire lofty sentiment and brilliant oratory; but when a Lincoln unbinds the shackles of a downtrodden race or when a Luther revolts in behalf of the fettered spirits of humanity and secures religious freedom for them, the outward action of these emancipators reveals a beauty of soul never discernible in those who soar in cloudland, but fear to soil their hands by actual work in the temple of humanity. The latter are not true temple- builders and would be unable to gain inspiration from the sight of that wonderful temple described by Manson in "The Servant in the House." The author calls him "Man-son;" this may mean that he regards him as the Son of Man, but it may also be that he meant Mason, for the Servant in the House was also a temple-builder. It is wonderful what insight the author of the play must have had when he planned the scene where his servant, the workman in love with his work, tells the worldly minded Churchman, who is full of platitudes and as vile as a whited sepulcher, of the temple which he, the workman, built. This conception is a mystic gem and we append it for the reader's meditation:

"I am afraid you may not consider it an altogether substantial concern. It has to be seen in a certain way, under certain conditions. SOME PEOPLE NEVER SEE IT AT ALL. You must understand this is no dead pile of stones and unmeaning timber; IT IS A LIVING THING.

"When you enter it you hear a sound--a sound as of some mighty poem chanted. Listen long enough and you will hear that it is made up of the beating of human hearts, of the nameless music of men's souls, that is, if you have ears. If you have eyes you will presently see the church itself, a looming mystery of many shapes and shadows leaping sheer from floor to dome, the WORK OF NO ORDINARY BUILDER.

"The pillars of it go up like the brawny trunks of heroes; the sweet human flesh of men and women is molded about its bulwarks, strong, impregnable. The faces of little children laugh out from every cornerstone; the terrible spans and arches of it are the joined hands of comrades; and up in the heights and spaces are inscribed the numberless musings of all the dreamers in the world.

It is yet building, building and built upon. Sometimes the work goes forward in deep darkness, sometimes in blinding light, now beneath the burden of unutterable anguish, now to the tune of great laughter and heroic shoutings like the cry of thunder. Sometimes in the silence of the night time one may hear the tiny hammerings of the comrades at work in the dome--THE COMRADES THAT HAVE GONE ALOFT."

It is such a temple that the Mystic Mason is building. He endeavors to WORK on the temple of Humanity at large, but since "when the rose adorns itself, it adorns the garden," he aims also to cultivate his own spiritual powers, as foreshadowed in THE MOLTEN SEA.

Solomon had already sued for the hand of the Queen of Sheba, and had been accepted, so, feeling that the meeting with Hiram Abiff might change her affections, he endeavored to consummate their marriage before granting her wish to meet the Grand Master. But the Queen was obstinate, she sensed the grandeur of the Master Workman whose skill had wrought the marvelous Temple and she felt intuitively drawn towards this man of action, as she had never been moved by the wisdom of Solomon, which only found verbal expression in flowery speeches and high ideals which he was unable to carry into realization. Therefore the reluctance of Solomon to let her meet Hiram Abiff made the Queen all the more anxious and importunate, so that at last Solomon was forced to accede to her request, and he grudgingly sent for the Grand Master. When Hiram Abiff appeared, and Solomon saw the love light kindle in the eyes of the Queen of Sheba, jealousy and hatred took root in his heart; he was, however, too wise to betray his feelings. But from that moment the plan of reconciliation and amalgamation of the Sons of Seth and the Sons of Cain which had been mapped out by the divine Hierarchies was doomed to failure, wrecked upon the rocks of jealousy and self-seeking.

The Queen of Sheba, according to the Masonic Legend, then requested Hiram Abiff to show her the workmen on the Temple. The Grand Master struck a nearby ROCK with his HAMMER so that the fire sparks flew, and at the sign of FIRE coupled with the work of power, the toilers of the Temple flocked around their Master in a great multitude, which no one could count, all ready and anxious to do his bidding. And this spectacle so impressed the Queen of Sheba with the wonderful power of this man that she determined to jilt Solomon and win the heart of Hiram Abiff. In other words, Humanity, when its eyes are opened to the impotence of the Churchmen, the Sons of Seth, who are themselves dependent upon divine favor, and when it sees the power and potency of the rulers of temporal fame is then ready to rush to them, and leave the spiritual for the material. This from the Microcosmic angle of matter.

From the Cosmic angle or view point we note again that Solomon's Temple is the Solar Universe and Hiram Abiff, the Grand Master, is the Sun which travels around the twelve signs of the Zodiac, enacting there the mystic drama of the Masonic Legend. At the Vernal Equinox the Sun leaves the WATERY SIGN OF PISCES, which is also feminine and docile, for the belligerent, martial, energetic, FIERY SIGN ARIES, the ram or lamb, where it is exalted in power. It fills the universe with a creative fire which is immediately seized upon by the innumerable billions of nature spirits who therewith build the Temple of the coming year in forest and fen. The forces of fecundation applied to the countless seeds slumbering in the ground causes them to germinate and fill the earth with luxuriant vegetation while the group spirit mate the beasts and birds in their charge so that they may bring forth and increase sufficiently to keep the fauna of our planet at normal. According to the Masonic Legend, Hiram Abiff, the Grand Master, used a hammer to call his workmen, and it is significant that the symbol of the sign Aries, where this wonderful creative activity commences, is shaped like a double ram's horn, which also resembles a hammer. It is also worthy of notice that in the ancient Norse Mythology, the Vanir or water deities are said to have been conquered by the Assir, or fire gods. The hammer wherewith the Norse God Thor struck fire from the sky finds its counterpart in the thunderbolt of Jove; like Hiram, the Assir belong to the Hierarchy of Fire, the Lucifer Spirits, THE SONS OF CAIN, striving for positive Mastership through individual effort, and therefore upholding the MALE ideal, which is diametrically opposite to that of the hierarchy which works in the plastic element Water. In the present day Temples of the latter Order, magic water stands at the door, and all who enter are required to apply this lethal liquid to the point in the forehead where the Spirit resides; their reason is drowned in dictums and dogmas, and the FEMALE ideal is worshipped in the Virgin Mary. Faith is the prime factor in their salvation, the attitude of unquestioning childlike obedience being cultivated.

It is different in the Temple of the other Order; when the candidate enters there, "poor," "naked" and "blind," he is asked at once what he is seeking, and when he answers "LIGHT," it is the duty of the Master to give what he asks and make him a PHREE MESSEN--a Child of Light. It is his duty also to teach him to work, and A MALE IDEAL, HIRAM ABIFF, the Master Workman, is presented for emulation. He is taught to be always ready to give a reason for his faith. As he qualifies in the work, he rises step by step, and at each degree more light is given. There are 3x3 degrees in the lesser Mysteries; when the candidate has passed the 9th Arch, he is in the Holy of Holies, which forms the gate to greater fields beyond the scope of Masonry. For further elucidation of that subject the student is referred to the chapters on Initiation, Volcanic Eruption and the number 9 in the *Rosicrucian Cosmo-Conception*.

Advancement and promotion in Mystic Masonry is not dependent on favor; it cannot be given till it has been earned and the candidate has stored in himself the power to rise, any more than a pistol can be fired till it has been loaded. INITIATION IS MERELY LIKE PULLING THE TRIGGER, and consists in showing the candidate how to use the power latent within himself.

There were some among the workmen on the Temple who thought they ought to be promoted to a higher degree, but who had not the power within; therefore Hiram Abiff could not initiate them, and as they were unable to see that the lack was in themselves, they felt provoked at Hiram, as over-ambitious candidates of today feel slighted and stamp a spiritual teacher a fraud who is unable to give them immediate illumination and induction into the invisible, while they are still eating of the "flesh-pots of Egypt," and unwilling to sacrifice themselves upon the altar of self-denial. The dissatisfied among Hiram's men entered into a conspiracy to spoil his great Masterpiece, the Molten Sea.

PART IV
CASTING THE MOLTEN SEA

As the spiritual gifts of the SONS OF SETH flowered in Solomon, the wisest of men, and enabled him to conceive and design a marvelous temple, according to the plan of his creator, Jehovah, so Hiram, the clever craftsman, embodied within himself the consummate skill of a long line of ancestral artificers. He possessed the concentrated quintessence of the material knowledge gained by the SONS OF CAIN, while they wrought from the wilderness of the world a concrete civilization; and in the execution of the wonderful Temple of Solomon this superlative skill found full fruition.

Thus this glorious edifice was the chef d'oeurve of both lines, an embodiment of the sublime spirituality of the CHURCHMEN, the SONS OF SETH, combined with the superlative skill of THE CRAFTSMEN, THE SONS OF CAIN. So far, the honors were even, the achievement equal. Solomon was contented; he had carried out the design transmitted to him, he had a place of worship worthy of the Lord he revered; but the soul of Hiram was not satisfied. Armed with the art of ages, he had constructed an incomparable masterpiece in architecture. BUT THE DESIGN HAD NOT BEEN HIS OWN; he had been merely the tool of an unseen architect, Jehovah, working through an intermediary Solomon. This rankled in his heart, for it was as necessary for him to originate as to breathe.

In that ancient age when Cain and Abel first found themselves upon earth, Abel contentedly cared for the flocks CREATED like himself and his parents, Adam and Eve, by Jehovah; but in Cain, semi-divine progeny of the Lucifer Spirit, Samael, and Eve, the creature of Jehovah, divine incentive to ORIGINAL EFFORT burned; he tilled the field and made two blades of grass grow where one grew before; the creative instinct must have expression.

Hiram, being the focus of and having inherited all the CRAFTS OF CAIN, was also invested with the Spirit of Samael intensified in commensurate ratio; therefore he was consumed by an overpowering urge to add something to the Temple that would eclipse the rest of the structure in beauty and importance. Out of the travail of his spirit was born the conception of THE MOLTEN SEA, and this great ideal he proceeded to carry into execution, though heaven and earth held their breath in awe at the audacity of his purpose.

The Bible gives very little information about the molten sea. In Second Chronicles, the fourth chapter, we learn that Hiram made such a vessel, that it was of considerable size, that it stood upon 12 oxen arranged so that their heads were at the periphery of this circular basin and their hind parts were towards its center. It was intended solely for use by the priests. Much is said of a nature to bewilder the reader, but the above salient points prove the signal importance of this instrument, as we shall see when we study and compare the Masonic account with this veiled word of the Bible. The Masonic story runs as follows:

When Hiram had about completed the Temple, he commenced to cast the various vessels required in the service according to designs made by Solomon as agent of Jehovah. Chief among these was the great laver, intended to hold the bath of purification, through which all priests must pass to enter the service of the Lord. This, and all the lesser vessels were successfully cast by Hiram, as recorded in the Bible. But there is an important distinction between the vessel and the molten sea which it was designed by Hiram to contain, and until that had been successfully poured, the vessel was without virtue, so far as purifying properties were concerned; until then it could no more cleanse the sin-stained soul than could a dry basin be utilized to cleanse the body. Nor could Solomon speak the Word, the formula for this wonderful work. None but Hiram knew it. This work was to be his Masterpiece, and IF HE SUCCEEDED, HIS ART WOULD HAVE LIFTED HIM ABOVE THE HUMAN, and made him divine like the Elohim Jehovah. In the garden of Eden, his divine progenitor Samael, had assured his mother, Eve; that she might become "as the Elohim," if she ate of the tree of knowledge. For ages his ancestors had wrought in the world; through the accumulated skill of the Sons of Cain, an edifice had been reared, wherein Jehovah hid himself "behind the veil" and communed only with his chosen priests, the Sons of Seth. THE SONS OF CAIN WERE THRUST OUT OF THE TEMPLE WHICH THEY HAD BUILT, as their father, Cain, had been driven from the garden which he had tilled. This Hiram felt to be an outrage and an injustice; so he applied himself to prepare the means whereby the Sons of Cain might "rend the veil" and open the way to God for "whosoever will."

To this end he sent messengers over the world to collect all the metals with which the Sons of Cain had ever wrought. With his hammer he pulverized them and placed them in a fiery furnace to extract by alchemistry, from each particle, the quintessence of knowledge derived in the experience of working with it. Thus the combined quintessence of these various BASE METALS would form a SPIRITUAL SUBLIMATE OF KNOWLEDGE incomparable in potency, valuable beyond all earthly things. Being of ultimate purity it would contain no color, but resemble a "sea of glass." Whoever should lave in it would find himself endowed with perpetual youth. No philosopher could compare with him in wisdom; this "white stone" knowledge would even enable him to lift the veil of invisibility and meet the superhuman Hierarchs, who work in the world with a potency undreamt of by the masses.

Masonic traditions tell us that Hiram's preparations were so perfect that success would have been assured, had not treachery triumphed. But the incompetent craftsmen whom Hiram had been unable to initiate into the higher degrees, conspired to pour WATER into the vessel cast to receive the Molten Sea; for they knew that the Son of Fire was unskilled in the manipulation of the watery element, and could not combine it with his wonderful alloy. Thus, by frustrating Hiram's cherished plan and spoiling his Masterpiece, they aimed to revenge themselves upon the Master. Solomon had been privately informed of the nefarious plot, but jealousy on account of the Queen of Sheba bound his tongue and stayed his arm, for he hoped that when the ambitious plan of Hiram failed, the affections of the queen would turn from his humiliated rival to himself. He therefore closed eyes and ears to plot and plotters.

When Hiram confidently PULLED THE PLUGS, the liquid fire rushed out, was met by the water, and there was a roar that seemed to shake heaven and earth, while the elements boiled and battled. All but Hiram hid their faces at the awful havoc; then from the center of the raging fire he heard the call of Tubal Cain, bidding him jump into the Molten Sea. Full of faith in his ancestor, who had gone before him upon the path of fire, Hiram obeyed and plunged fearlessly into the flames. Sinking through the disintegrated bottom of the vessel, he was conducted successfully through NINE-ARCH-LIKE layers of the earth to the Center, where he found himself in the presence of Cain, the founder of his family, who gave him instructions relative to blending Water and Fire, and who furnished him with a NEW HAMMER AND A NEW WORD, which would enable him to produce these results. Cain looked into the future and uttered a prophecy which has been partially fulfilled; what remains is in process of realization day by day, and as surely as time goes on all will come to pass.

"You, Hiram," said Cain, "are destined to die with hopes unfulfilled, but many sons will be born to the widow and keep your memory green through the ages, and at length one will come who is greater than you. You shall not wake till the Lion of Judah raises you with the powerful grip of His paw. This day you have received your BAPTISM OF FIRE, but He shall BAPTIZE YOU WITH WATER AND WITH SPIRIT; you, and every son of the widow, who will come to Him. Greater than Solomon, he will build a new city and a Temple wherein the nations may worship. The Sons of Cain and the Sons of Seth shall there meet in Peace, at the sea of glass. And as Melchisedec, King of Salem (Salem means Peace,) and Priest of God, ministered to Abraham, the father of nations, when mankind was yet in its infancy, so shall this new Light combine in Himself the dual office of King and Priest after the order of Melchisedec. He shall judge the nations with THE LAW OF LOVE and to him that overcometh will be given a White Stone with a name that will serve as passport to the temple. There he may meet the king FACE TO FACE.

Hiram was again conducted to the surface of the earth and as he walked from the scene of his shattered ambition, the conspirators set upon and fatally wounded him; but before he expired, he hid the hammer and disc upon which he had inscribed the Word. This was never found until ages later when Hiram, "the widow's Son," was reborn as Lazarus and became the friend and pupil of the Lion of Judah, who raised him from death through initiation. When the hammer was found it had the shape of a CROSS, and the disc had become a ROSE. Therefore Hiram took his place among the immortals under the new and symbolical name Christian Rosenkreuz. He founded the Order of Temple-Builders which bears his name; in that Order aspiring souls are still instructed how to fuse the base metals and make the White Stone. The symbology of the foregoing will be explained in the following chapters.

PART V
THE MYSTERY OF MELCHISEDEC

Among all the characters mentioned in the Bible none is more mysterious than Melchisedec; said to be without father, mother, or earthly kin, and holding the dual office of king and priest. Paul in his epistle to the Hebrews gives us most information showing the connection between Christ and Melchisedec, both of them Kings and High Priests, but of different dispensations.

"God who at sundry times and in diverse manners spake in times past unto the fathers by the Prophets has in these last days spoken unto us by His Son whom He has appointed heir of all things, by whom also He made the worlds. * * * No man taketh this honor unto himself but he that is called of God, as was Aaron. So also Christ glorified not Himself to be made a High Priest, but He that said unto Him 'Thou art my Son, today have I begotten Thee.' As He saith also in another place, Thou art a Priest for The Age after the order of Melchisedec, who in the days of his flesh when he had offered up prayers and supplications with strong crying and tears unto Him that was able to save him from death and was heard in that He feared though He were a son, yet learned He obedience by the things He suffered; and being made perfect, He became author of eternal salvation unto all that obey Him; called of God a High Priest after the order of Melchisedec, of whom we have many things to say and hard to be uttered. * * * For this Melchisedec, king of Salem, priest of the Most High God, who met Abraham returning from the slaughter of kings and blessed him; to whom also Abraham gave a tenth part of all, first being by interpretation king of righteousness and after that also king of Salem, which is king of peace; without father, without mother, without ancestors, having neither beginning of days nor end of life but made like unto the Son of God, abideth a priest continually. * * * And here men that die (the Levites) receive tithes, but there he receiveth them of whom it is witnessed the He liveth. * * * If, therefore, perfection were by the law and its priesthood what further need was there that another priest should rise after the order of Melchisedec and not be called after the order of Aaron? * * * For it is evident that our Lord sprang out of Judah of which tribe Moses spake nothing concerning the priesthood. And it is yet far more evident for that after the similitude of Melchisedec there ariseth another priest who is made not after the law of carnal commandments but after the power of an endless life, for he testifies 'Thou are a priest for The Age, after the order of Melchisedec.' * * * By so much was Jesus made the surety of a better testament; * * * because He continueth ever and has an Age lasting priesthood; * * * for the law maketh men High Priests who have infirmities, but the Word of God which was since the law, maketh the Son who is consecrated for evermore. Now of the things which we have spoken this is the sum; we have such a high Priest who is yet on the right hand of the throne of the Majesty in the Heavens, a minister of the sanctuary and of the true tabernacle, which the Lord made and not man. * * * Almost all things in the heavens should be purified with these, but the heavenly things themselves were better sacrifices than these, for Christ is not entered into the holy place made with hands which are the figures of the true, but into Heaven itself, now to appear in the presence of God for us; * * * and now has He obtained a more excellent ministry by how much also He is mediator of a better covenant which was established upon better promises; for if the first covenant had been perfect then there should be no place for a second. But finding fault with the old He saith 'Behold the days come when I will make a new covenant with the house of Israel and with the house of Judah, not according to the covenant that I made with their fathers in the day when I took them by the hand and led them out of the land of Egypt, because they continued not in my covenant, and I regarded them not, 'saith the Lord. * * * For this is the covenant that I will make to the House of Israel after those days, saith the Lord. 'I WILL PUT MY LAWS INTO THEIR MINDS AND WRITE THEM IN THEIR HEARTS, and I will be to them a God and they shall be to me a people and THEY SHALL NOT TEACH EVERY MAN HIS NEIGHBOR and every man his brother saying, Know the Lord, for ALL SHALL KNOW ME FROM THE LEAST TO THE GREATEST.'"

The foregoing quotations from Paul's Epistle to the Hebrews are not found there consecutively as here arranged. It is necessary to intelligently piece the Bible narrative together so that we may obtain an outline of the future development which has been sketched out by the divine Hierarchs to constitute our evolution. Comprehension of this plan is essential to the correct understanding of the Cosmic relationship of Freemasonry and Catholicism; it is also necessary to fully appreciate the purpose of the Molten Sea and to learn how to intelligently make this wonderful alloy. As Paul says, these things are hard to say, but we shall make an attempt to present the mysteries of Melchisedec and the Molten Sea in plain language so that we may aid in the expressed purpose of the Bible to enlighten all men, that all shall know from the least to the greatest what is the purpose of evolution, and thus give them a chance to align themselves with the trend of Cosmic events.

To understand the mystery of Melchisedec we must revert to the earlier epochs of man's stay upon the earth during the age called the Hyperborean Epoch. The earth was then in an extremely heated condition. Man in the making was then double sexed, male-female, like so many of our present plants, and he also resembled the plants in being inert and lacking in desire and aspirations. At that time man was the tractable ward of the Divine Hierarchs who guided him physically, these being darkly referred to in the Bible as "Kings of Edom." Later, during the Lemurian Epoch, when the body of man had crystallized and condensed somewhat more, mankind was divided into sexes physically. But as the consciousness of man was still focused in the spiritual world they were unconscious of the physical act of generation, as we are now of digestion; neither did they know birth or death and were in fact totally unaware of the possession of a physical vehicle until in time they sensed it during the generative process; it was then said that "Adam KNEW Eve." At that time Lucifer Spirits, fallen Angels and inhabitants of the warlike planet Mars, taught them how to eat of the TREE OF KNOWLEDGE, which is the symbolical name for the generative act. Thus by degrees their eyes were opened and they became aware of the physical world, but lost touch with the spiritual and the Guardian Angels who had previously been their benevolent guides. Only a few of the most spiritual among them retained their higher vision and communion with the Divine Hierarchs. These were then known as prophets, who acted as messengers between the invisible divine leaders and their respective peoples. But in time mankind desired to select its own leaders and demanded visible kings; at least we know that the Israelites repudiated the divine ruler ship and demanded a king, and thus Saul was appointed. Then the dual office of Ruler and Priest, including temporal and spiritual leadership, was also divided, for no man sufficiently versed in worldly matters to fill the office of king efficiently, had been found holy enough to also undertake the spiritual leadership of his brethren, and vice versa. A true priest, able to lead his flock spiritually, cannot also beneficently dominate their physical fortunes as ruler of a temporal domain. For as STATECRAFT, in its highest phase, aims to rule the masses with an eye single to their physical welfare, and PRIESTCRAFT, benevolently exercised, seeks to guide them solely for the soul's progress, so conflict must of necessity follow this separation, even though both the spiritual and temporal rulers be actuated by the highest and most unselfish motives. Melchisedec was the symbolical name of the divine Hierarchs who filled the dual office of king and priest; in the guidance of their double-sexed charges and while they reigned there was peace on earth, but as soon as the offices of king and priest were divorced and the sexes divided, it is not surprising for the reasons given above that the peaceful reign of Melchisedec has been followed by an age of war and strife, such strife as has been experienced during the present dispensation. Formerly the unifying factors of a dual office in the ruler and the double sex of his people precluded the clashing of interests which now obtains, and which will continue until another divine ruler shall present himself to embody within in his own person the qualifications of the dual office of king and priest after the order of Melchisedec, and until sex generation be abolished. In this connection it is significant that the Bible narrative begins in the Garden of Eden, where mankind were male-female and innocent; then in the next chapter we are told of the division of sexes, the transgression of the command not to eat of the Tree of Knowledge, and the infliction of the penalty--painful parturition and swift death. From then on the Old Testament tells of war, struggle and strife and in the last chapter makes the prophecy that there shall a Sun of righteousness arise with healing in his wings.

Then the New Testament opens with an account of the birth of Christ, who proclaimed a kingdom of heaven which is to be established. He is later called King and Priest after the order of Melchisedec, uniting within himself THE DUAL OFFICE. It is also said that in heaven there will be neither marrying nor giving in marriage, for the SOMA PSUCHICON, or soul-body, which Paul tells us is the vehicle we shall use in the kingdom of heaven (First Corinthians, fifteenth chapter), is not liable to death and decay. Thus there will be no death, and birth of bodies like those generated in wedlock would be superfluous, for Paul tells us that flesh and blood cannot inherit the kingdom of God. Hence marriage will be unnecessary, the clashing of interests due to the lust of sex and the love of power will then disappear and the love of souls will be hallowed by the spirit of peace.

Thus it is plain that the Sons of Cain with their followers, the CRAFTSMEN, and the Sons of Seth with their retinue, the CHURCHMEN, must finally merge and be unified in the Kingdom of Christ. We have already seen how Hiram Abiff, the Widow's Son, left his father, the Lucifer Spirit Samael, after the BAPTISM OF FIRE in the Molten Sea, and how he received the mission to prepare the way for the kingdom among the Sons of Cain, his brethren, by developing their arts and crafts as temple builders--Masons-- and teaching them the preparation of the Philosopher's Stone or Molten Sea. Thus also the physically negative Sons of Seth must learn to leave their father, Jehovah, and naturally the first to take the step must be a great soul.

As the superlative skill of the Sons of Cain was focused in Hiram Abiff at the time of his baptism of fire, so the sublime spirituality of the Sons of Seth was centered in Jesus at the time of His BAPTISM IN THE WATERS of Jordan. When He arose from this water He was in the same position as Hiram emerging from the fire; each had left his father respectively, Jehovah and Samael, and each was ready to serve the Christ. Therefore the Christ Spirit was seen at the Baptism to descend upon Jesus' body, which was inhabited and used by Christ during His ministry. Jesus himself, the spirit, left that body and was given a mission to serve the churches while his body was being used for direct teaching by the Christ, and his blood was being prepared as an OPEN SESAME to the Kingdom of God, a Panacea to be used by His brethren, the Sons of Seth, in the same manner that the Molten Sea serves the Sons of Cain. In the Epistle of the Hebrews where Paul gives us a few hints concerning the Mystery of Melchisedec in the character of High Priest, he emphasized the absolute necessity of blood as an adjunct to the Temple Service; he show how the High Priest was required to offer blood for his own sins before he was qualified to give sacrifice also for sins of the people, and that this double sacrifice must be performed year after year. He points to the sacrifice upon Golgotha as having been made ONCE AND FOR ALL, providing a way of atonement through the blood of Jesus. During the regime of Jehovah, the blood of humanity had become impregnated with egotism, which is the separative factor in this age. From this sin it must be cleansed before mankind can be united and enter the Kingdom of Christ. This was a gigantic task, for humanity had become so impregnated with selfishness that scarcely anyone would do another a favor. Hence the post- mortem panorama, of life at the time of Christ contained nothing that would give a life in the First Heaven or make for spiritual progress. Almost all the post-mortem existence of the people was spent in the purgatorial expiration of their wrong-doings, and even their Second Heaven life, where man learns to do creative work was almost barren. Then Solomon, the King, was again called into the arena of life to perform a mission for the benefit and welfare of his brethren, the Sons of Seth; he was peculiarly fitted for this work because at heart he was unselfish as shown by the request which he made at the time when Jehovah appeared to him in a dream and asked what he would have as a gift when he ascended the throne. Solomon then said unto God "Thou hast shown great mercy unto David my father and hath made me to reign in his stead now; now, O Lord, let thy promise unto David my father be established, for Thou hast made me king over a people like the dust of the earth in multitude. GIVE ME NOW WISDOM AND KNOWLEDGE, that I may go out and come in before this people, for who can judge Thy people that is so great?" And God said to Solomon: "Because this was in thine heart and thou hast not asked riches, wealth or honor, nor the life of thine enemies, neither hast ye asked long life, but hast asked wisdom and knowledge for thyself that thou mayest judge my people over whom I have made thee king, wisdom and knowledge is granted unto thee, and I will give thee riches and wealth and honor such as none of the kings have had that have been before thee, neither shall there any after thee have the like."

It was this characteristic of unselfishness developed in former lives that fitted the spirit of Solomon which inhabited the body of Jesus for the high mission it was destined to fulfill; to serve as a vehicle for the unifying unselfish Christ Spirit, for the purpose of bringing to an end the division between the Sons of Seth and the Sons of Cain and uniting them in the Brotherhood forming the kingdom of heaven.

When Faust made the pact with Mephistopheles, as recorded in the ancient soul-myth of that name, he was about to sign it in ink but Mephisto says: "No, sign it in blood." For this request Faust asks the reason and Mephistopheles says knowingly and cunningly "BLOOD IS A MOST PECULIAR ESSENCE!" It is said in the Bible that the blood of bulls and calves will not take away sins and that is reasonable, but how then about the blood of Jesus, which is extolled as a panacea? To understand this great mystery of Golgotha it is necessary to study the composition and the function of the flood from the occult point of view.

When blood is placed under a microscope, it appears as a number of minute globules or discs, but when seen by the trained clairvoyant as it courses through the living body blood is found to be a gas, a spiritual essence. The heat is caused by the Ego which is within that blood, for as the Bible says, the LIFE is in the blood. Mephisto was right when he said that it is a most peculiar essence, for it contains the Ego, and whoever wants to obtain a power over the Ego must have his blood.

The human Ego is more powerful than the group spirit of the animal, as we can see when we apply the scientific test known as haemolysis. Strange blood of a higher animal will kill, if inoculated into the veins of a lower species; if we take human blood and inject it into an animal, the animal will be unable to endure the high vibration that is in the blood of the human being and it will die. On the other hand a human being may be inoculated with the blood of a lower animal without injury. In ancient times it was strictly forbidden anyone belonging to one tribe to marry into another tribe because it was known then by the leaders of humanity that the strange blood would kill something; it always does. We read that Adam and Methuselah lived so many centuries; at that time it was the custom to marry in the family, marry as closely as possible, so that the tie of blood might be as strong as it could be made. Then the blood that coursed through the veins of the people in that family contained the pictures of all that had happened to the different ancestor; these were stored in the mind which is now subconscious. Then they were consciously and constantly before the inner vision of all people, and each family was united by this common blood wherein the pictures of their ancestors lived. The sons saw the life of their fathers, and thus the fathers lived in the sons; and since the consciousness of Adam and Methuselah and the other Patriarchs lived for centuries in their descendants, they were said to live personally.

It was then as great a crime to marry OUTSIDE the family as it now is to marry within. Even among the early Norsemen, we learn that if anyone wanted to marry within a strange family, he was first obliged to mix blood; it must first be tested to see whether his blood would mix with that of the family into which he desired to marry. And thus haemolysis was known to many in some of its phases at least. If the blood did not mix, it would bring about "CONFUSION OF CASTE," as the Hindu says; a straight line of descent must be kept, for otherwise those pictures in the inner vision would become mixed and would be confused. This marrying in the family or tribe was what engendered the selfishness, the clannishness, and the struggle and strife of the world. To break these up, the practice must be discontinued; thus when Christ came He advocated the discontinuance of the practice when He said: "Before Abraham was, I AM." In effect He said: I do not care for the race father, but I glory in the I Am, the Ego that was long before he was. And He also said: "Who does not leave father and mother cannot follow Me." As long as you are tied to the family, the nation, the tribe, you are siding with the old blood, the old ways, and cannot amalgamate into a universal brotherhood. That can only come when people marry internationally because when there are so many nations the way to unite them is through marriage. Let Abraham, the race and tribe father, die; let the "I AM" LIVE. Christ knew the occult fact that the mixture of blood in international marriage always kills something; if it does not kill the body, it kills something else. If we mate a horse and a donkey, the outcome is a HYBRID, the mule; in that mule something is missing on account of the mixture of strange blood, namely, the faculty of propagation which is lacking in all hybrids. Similarly when we marry internationally something else is destroyed and that is the pictures in the inner vision. The different pictures of different families clash. And so the clairvoyance, the touch with the spiritual world, with the memory of Nature, has waned since the practice of marrying in the tribe was broken up. The Highland Scot who marries in the clan and the gypsies alone retain this second sight in a measure. Thus we see that the blood is now differently constituted from what it was in the earlier ages of human evolution. The body of Jesus was a pioneer vehicle of superlative purity at the time when the Christ Spirit entered it, as a means of ingress to the center of the earth by the identical path which he jumped into the Molten Sea and was conducted along the path of Initiation to the center of the earth where Cain, his ancestor, dwelt.

This journey of Christ is recorded in I Peter 3:18-19 after Christ had been freed from the flesh by the violent death on Golgotha. When anyone is killed, the venous blood with its impurities clings closely to the flesh, and therefore the arterial blood which flows is distinctly cleaner than it would otherwise be; it is more free from passion and desire. And being etherealized by the great Christ Spirit, THE CLEANSED BLOOD OF JESUS OVERFLOWED THE WORLD, PURIFIED THE ETHERIC REGION OF SELFISHNESS TO A GREAT EXTENT, and gave man a better chance to draw to himself materials which will allow him to form altruistic purposes and desires. Thus the age of altruism was there inaugurated. By faith in this blood, and by imitation of the Christ Life the Sons of Seth are therefore provided with a means of purging from themselves the curse of selfishness; while the Sons of Cain were given the emblem of the ROSE AND THE CROSS to teach them to work faithfully to make the Molten Sea, the Philosopher's Stone, and to find the NEW WORD which shall admit them to the kingdom, for they believe more in works than in faith.

The accompanying chart shows graphically the three Ages mentioned in this article:

(1) THE FIRST AGE, when each human being was a complete creative unit, male-female, double sexed, and ruled by one Hierarch, Melchisedec, who filled a dual office as King and Priest.

(2) THE SECOND AGE, when the division of the race into men and women, and the division of the rulership into State and Church caused war and strife.

THE STATE espouses the cause of FATHERHOOD AND MAN and upholds the male ideal of Arts, Crafts and Industry, embodied in Hiram Abiff.

THE CHURCH espouses the cause of MOTHERHOOD AND WOMAN and holds aloft the female ideal of love, and hearth and home embodied in the Madonna and her child.

It is the conflicting interests of the man and the woman, the home and the shop, the Church and the State, which cause the economic struggle, the war and the strife with which mankind is cursed and which make all long and pray for the reign of peace.

(3) THE THIRD AGE, when a divine Christ, who, like Melchisedec, shall fill the dual office of King and Priest, and shall rule over a urged and glorified humanity, which has risen from sex-love to soul-love.

PART VI
SPIRITUAL ALCHEMY

When we expose a piece of iron to the air, the oxygen contained in the latter element oxidizes the iron and in time disintegrates it. This process is commonly known as rusting. The blood comes in contact with the air every time it passes through the lungs, and as a needle is drawn to a magnet, so does the oxygen of the inspired air coalesce with the iron the blood. A process of combustion takes place, which is similar to the rusting or oxidation we observed in the iron exposed to the air.

The ether contained in the dense fiber of wood, after the latter has undergone combustion in a stove, passes outwards through the iron in the form of semi-invisible heat-waves vibrating at different velocities according to the degree of heat in the furnace. So the spiritual vibration generated by the combustion of oxygen and iron in our physical bodies, passes outwards and colors our invisible vehicles according to their vibratory pitch. Low vibrations are seen as red, the higher are yellow, and the highest blue. Experience has taught us that combustible material may be placed in a furnace and all conditions necessary to combustion may be present but that until the match is applied the materials remain unconsumed. Those who have studied the laws of combustion know also that a forced draft carries with it great quantities of oxygen which is necessary to obtain heat from fuel containing much mineral. The reason for this condition lies in the fact that minerals, being the lowest in the scale of evolution, vibrate at a correspondingly slower rate than the plant, animal or man. It requires a maximum effort to raise their vibrations to such a pitch that combustion may liberate their spiritual essence, and oxygen is the accelerator in this process. Were the same amount of oxygen supplied to good vegetable fuel, which naturally vibrates at a higher rate than mineral, the furnace would be in danger of destruction because of the intensity of the heat generated.

A similar process takes place within the body, which is the temple of the spirit; this is the flame which kindles the inner fire and generates the spiritual product which passes outwards from all warm-blooded creatures as heat radiates from a stove. (Cold-blooded creatures are so low in the scale of evolution that they have as yet no life WITHIN themselves but are worked upon by the group-spirit from without entirely and it is the group-spirit which generates the lifegiving currents responsible for the animation in these creatures; these currents pass INWARDS to sustain the nascent life until it shall be able to respond and begin to send currents outwards from itself.) These radiant lines of force emanating invisibly to the physical sight from our dense bodies are our aura, as already stated, and while the color of each individual's aura differs from that of all other individuals there is nevertheless a basic or ground color showing its status in the scale of evolution. In the lower races this ground color is a dull RED like the color of a slow burning fire, indicating their passionate, emotional nature. When we examine people upon a somewhat higher rung of the ladder of evolution, the basic color or vibration radiated by them is seen to be of an ORANGE hue, the yellow of intellect mixed with the red of passion. By the spiritual alchemy unconsciously performed by them as they travel along the path of progress and learn to make their emotions subservient to mind a measure, through many experiences in the school of life, they are gradually freeing themselves from bondage to the martial Lucifer Spirits and the War God Jehovah, whose colors are scarlet and red; also by obeying consciously or unconsciously the unifying altruistic Christ Spirit whose vibrations produce a YELLOW color which is thus mingling with the red and will gradually obliterate it. The golden aureole painted by the artists gifted with spiritual sight around holy men is a physical representation of a spiritual promise which applies to Humanity as a whole, though it has only been realized by a few who are called Saints. After lives of battle with their passions, after patient persistence in well-doing, high aspirations and steadfast adherence to lofty purposes these people have raised themselves above the red ray and are now entirely imbued with the golden Christ ray and its vibration. This spiritual fact has been embodied by mediaeval artists gifted with spiritual sight, in their pictures of saints whom they represent as surrounded by a golden aureole, indicating their emancipation from the power of the Lucifer Spirits of Mars who are the fallen angels, as well as from Jehovah and His angels, who belong to an earlier stage of evolution and are warders of national and race religions. The Lucifer spirits find expression in the iron in our blood. Iron is a Mars metal, difficult to start into high vibration, so difficult that it takes many lives of great effort to change the product of its combustion to the golden color which designates the Saint. When that has been achieved, the greatest feat of alchemy has been performed; THE BASE METAL HAS BEEN CHANGED TO GOLD, the wonderful alloy of the Molten Sea has been made from the dross of the earth. All that then remains is to "PULL THE PLUGS" and pour it. The natural golden color is the Christ ray finding its chemical expression in the oxygen, a solar element, and as we advance upon the path of evolution towards Universal Brotherhood even those who are not professedly religious acquire a tinge of gold in their auras due to the higher altruistic impulses common to the West. Paul speaks of this as "Christ being formed IN YOU," for when we have learned to mix the alloy by spiritual lives, when we vibrate to the same pitch as He, we are Christ-like, ready, as said, to pull the plugs of the crucibles and to pour the Molten Sea. Christ was liberated on the cross through spiritual centers located where the nails are said to have been driven, and elsewhere. And one who has prepared the Molten Sea is also instructed by the Teacher how to pull the plugs and soar into the higher spheres or, as the Masonic saying is, to "TRAVEL IN FOREIGN COUNTRIES."

This is in harmony with the dictum of Christ that to become His disciple one must leave father and mother. That is one of the hard sayings of the Gospel and generally misunderstood because it is taken to refer to our physical father and mother in the present life, whereas in the esoteric point of view something very different was intended. To get the idea let us once more call to mind that the Lucifer spirits by the introduction of iron into the system made it possible for the human ego to become an INDWELLING spirit, but continued oxidation of the blood renders the body undesirable as a habitation in time and death ensues. Therefore, though the Lucifer spirits helped us into the body, they are also truly angels of death, and the progeny of Samael and Eve are subject thereto as well as the children begotten by her and Adam, for all are flesh.

The Sun is the center of life and rules the life-giving gas we know as oxygen which coalesces with the martial iron. Therefore, Christ, the Lord of the Sun, is also the Lord of Life, and when by spiritual alchemy as has been explained, we become like Him, we are immortal and thus we leave our father Samael and our mother Eve, and DEATH HAS NO MORE DOMINION OVER US. That does not mean that death may not happen to the body of such people, but the body entirely under their control, and a body used by such people usually lasts for many hundreds of years unless it becomes expedient to take another one. Then by the same process of spiritual alchemy they are able to create an adult body for themselves and to leave the old body which they desire to discard for the new one which they have made previously and fitted to serve their purpose. The question will now probably arise in the reader's mind: "How can an Initiate create such a new adult body, ready to wear, before he relinquishes his old one?" The answer to this question involves an understanding of the law of assimilation, but it should be said in the first place that no one who has just become aware of the spiritual world and perhaps learned to function in the soul-body only recently is capable of performing this feat. This requires a vastly more spiritual development, and only those who are very high in the scale of initiation at our present time are able to perform the feat. The method is, however, said to be as follows:

When food is taken into the body of anyone, be he Adept or ignoramus, the law of assimilation is that he must first overpower each particle and conform it to himself; he must subdue and conquer the individual cell life before it can become part of his body. When this has been done, the cell will stay with him for a longer or shorter time according to the constitution and place in evolution of the life that dwells within it. The cell composed of tissue that has once been incorporated in an animal body and interpenetrated by a desire body has the most evolved cell life, therefore this life quickly reasserts itself and leaves the body into which it has been temporarily assimilated. Hence one who lives upon a flesh diet must replenish his food supply very often; such material would therefore be unsuitable for the purpose of building a body that has to wait for some time before the Adept enters it. Food consisting of vegetables, fruits and nuts, particularly when these are ripe and fresh, is interpenetrated by a great deal of the ether which composes the vital body of the plant. These are much easier to subdue and to incorporate into the polity of the body, also they stay much longer there before the individual cell life can assert itself. Therefore the Adept who wished to build a body ready to wear before he leaves the old one, naturally builds it of fresh vegetables, fruits and nuts, taking them into the body which he uses daily where they become subjected to his will, a part of himself.

The soul-body of such a man is naturally very large and powerful; he separates a part of that and makes a mould or matrix into which he may build each day physical particles superfluous to the nourishment of the body he is using. Thus by degrees, having assimilated a considerable surplus of new material, he may also draw upon the vehicle he is wearing for material that can be incorporated in the new body. So in the course of some time he gradually transmutes one body into the other, and when the point is reached where emaciation of the old body would be observable to the outside world and cause comment, he would have balanced matters so that the new body is ready to wear, and he can step out of the old into the new. But he does not do that merely for the purpose of living in the same community. It is possible for him by reason of his great knowledge to use the same body for many centuries in such a manner that it would still seem young, for there is no wear and tear upon it such as we ordinary mortals cause by our passions, emotions and desires. But when he does create a new body it is always, as far as the writer knows, for the purpose of leaving the environment in which he is at that time and taking up his work in a new place. It is by reason of this fact that we hear of men like Cagliostro, Saint Germain and others who one day appeared in a certain environment, took up an important work and then disappeared. Nobody knew whence they had come or whither they had gone, but everybody that knew these people was ready to testify to their remarkable qualities, whether for the purpose of vilification or praise. This transition of the Adept from the dominion of death to the realm of immortality was foreshadowed in the daring leap of Hiram Abiff, the Grand Master-Workman of Solomon's Temple, into the seething sea of molten metal and his passage through the NINE arch-like strata of the earth which form the path of initiation; also in the baptism of Jesus and the subsequent descent from Golgotha into the subterranean region where his vital body is still kept awaiting the day of final egress of the Christ Spirit at the second advent. In our next chapter we shall follow Hiram Abiff along this path of initiation to the embodiment he wore at the time of Christ's appearance upon the earth, showing where and how he received the new initiation.

PART VII
THE PHILOSOPHER'S STONE: WHAT IT IS AND HOW IT IS MADE

Those who have studied the writings of the ancient alchemists have always been much mystified by what is said concerning the philosopher's stone and the process of transmuting the base metals into gold. These claims have naturally given rise to a great deal of vague speculation. From time to time, students have asked for a direct statement from the writer concerning this subject of paramount importance, and as we are standing upon the threshold of a new age where this precious jewel with all its power will be evolved and possessed by a considerable number of people, we feel that it is important to divest the subject of all the mystery that surrounds it and speak in plain terms concerning the matter. Then all who really wish to take the trouble involved, for it involves arduous labor, nothing worth having being ever gained without cost, may know how to make for themselves this great gem.

We are taught that in the beginning God created Heaven and Earth--the whole universe in fact, and we understand that this great creative force expresses itself either as WILL or IMAGINATION. By imagination the Great Architect of the Universe must first have visualized everything as it now is, or as it was first created, and then by His will the physical atoms were marshaled into this matrix of thought, thus gradually bringing the universe into manifestation as designed by its creator. Nor is this process complete, but will continue until the whole has become perfect as originally designed.

The divine Hierarchies who have carried out the plan of the great Creator also use the same dual creative force when fashioning the crystal in the mineral, the leaf of the plant, or the shape of the animal. Their powerful imagination pictures in the archetypal region of the earth that which they desire to create, and their concentrated will moulds the coarser matter into this matrix until it assumes a definite physical form as desired.

Man, the spirit, has a like creative power, and has through the ages, under the guidance of the Gods, learned to build bodies of increasing value as instruments for his expression. But his pilgrimage through matter was undertaken for the purpose of making him an independent creative intelligence, and to attain that end it was necessary that he should at the proper time, be emancipated from the guardianship of the Gods, so that he might learn to create, not only for himself, but also to aid and to teach others in the great School of Life.

During the course of his evolution, Man has become more and more enlightened concerning the mystery of Life; but nevertheless, it is only a few hundred years ago when life and liberty were endangered by the expression of opinions in advance of the commonly accepted views. It was for this reason that the alchemists who had studied more deeply that the majority, were forced to embody their teachings in highly allegorical and symbolical language. Their teaching concerning the spiritual evolution of man, and their use of the terms SALT, SULPHUR, MERCURY, and AZOTH, so mystifying to the masses, were nevertheless rooted in cosmic truths, highly illuminating to the Initiate. The students of the Rosicrucian teachings who have learned how the world came into being and the process of gradual creation should have no difficulty in properly understanding every part of the alchemist's language.

We know in the first place, that there was a time when Man-in-the-making was a hermaphrodite, male-female, and able to create from himself, and we remember also that at that time he was like the plant in other respects. His consciousness was like that which we possess in dreamless sleep and which is possessed by the plant. The vital energy which he absorbed into his body was used solely for the purpose of growing, until the time of propagation came, when a new budding body was cast off to grow also. There was no incentive to action, but if there had been, Man would have had no mind or will to direct it.

For the emancipation of humanity from this negative condition, one-half of the creative force was turned upward under the direction of the angels for the purpose of building a larynx and a brain, that man might learn to create by thought as do the divine Hierarchies, and express the creative thought in words. Thus man ceased to be physically hermaphrodite and became unisexual. He can no longer create from himself PHYSICALLY as do the hermaphrodite plants, nor PSYCHICALLY as do the Elohim, the male-female Hierarchs, in whose image he was originally made, and thus he occupies at the present time, an unenviable intermediate position between the plant and the God.

At the time when one half of the human sex force was diverted for the purpose of building a brain, men were helpless and lacking in knowledge of how to overcome conditions. They did not even have the consciousness to know that there was a difficulty, and had no outside help been given the race must have died out. Therefore the Angels from the Moon, who were the guardians of mankind, herded the sexes together in great temples at times when the interplanetary lines of force were propitious to propagation and thus they perpetuated the race. It was also proposed that when the brain had been completed, the Lords of Mercury, Elder Brothers of our present humanity who excelled in intelligence, should teach us how to use the mind and make it truly creative so that we would no longer be dependent upon the separate sexual process of generation now in vogue. Thus by the work of these two great Hierarchies, we were raised from unconsciousness to the first stage of creative intelligence, FROM PLANT TO GOD.

We have also learned that this plan was frustrated by the Lucifer Spirits, stragglers from the humanity of the Moon Period, who lived upon the planet Mars. They needed a physical field of action, but were unable to create one for themselves, hence for selfish reasons they taught humanity how by cooperation of the sexes a new body may be created at any time; and in order to give an incentive they instilled into mankind the animalistic passionate nature which we now possess.

Thus to the ancient alchemists, the Angels from the Moon which rules the saline tides of the sea were designated by the term "SALT." They had found that a certain amount of salt in the blood is necessary to the mental processes, also that excess salt in the blood produces insanity, as best proven by the experiences of shipwrecked sailors who become LUNATICS when they drink water containing the lunar element SALT. Thus also they established a connection between the Moon and mind.

The fiery Lucifer Spirits who have taken such a baneful part in man's evolution became associated with the fiery element "SULPHUR." The alchemists said that man is rendered unconscious and dies by continuous inhalation of this element; so man, the spirit, was rendered unconscious of and dead to the spiritual realms by the teachings which were instilled into him by the Lucifer Spirits.

The metal MERCURY, they contended, is the most elusive of all metals. It will penetrate and evaporate through most substances with which it is brought in contact; and therefore they likened it to the Lords of Mercury who are past masters in penetrating the secrets of nature by the mind. Mercury is also capable of freeing the spirit from its physical prison house.

By the process of GENERATION carried on at a propitious time under the guidance of the Angels, man was treading the path from plant to God, following the highway of evolution as originally planned.

From this path he strayed into the byways of DEGENERATION, led by the Lucifer Spirits, and is therefore now as it were in a slough from which he cannot extricate himself save with the help of others further advanced than he.

When this becomes apparent to him and he starts to search for light, he stands at the pathway of REGENERATION guarded by the Lords of Mercury who with their wisdom will guide him toward the desired goal. The method as outlined by the ancient alchemists we shall discuss when we have summed up in a few words the points made. These must be firmly fixed in mind to appreciate the full value of what follows.

The creative force used by God to bring a solar system into manifestation, and the force used by the divine Hierarchies to form the physical vehicle of the lower kingdoms over which they rule as group spirits, expresses itself in a dual manner as WILL and IMAGINATION, and is the same as the UNITED creative force of the male and the female which results in the creation of a human body. At one time man was bi-sexual, male-female, and therefore each was able to propagate his species without assistance from anyone else. But one-half of the creative force has been temporarily diverted upwards to build a brain and larynx in order to enable him sometime to create by his own mind, to form thoughts and speak the word of power that shall make his thoughts flesh. Three great creative Hierarchies were particularly concerned in bringing about this change: the ANGELS from the Moon, the MERCURIANS, and the LUCIFER SPIRITS from Mars.

The Alchemists connected the Angels from the Moon, which rules the saline tides, with the element SALT, the Lucifer Spirits from Mars with the element SULPHUR, and the Mercurians with the metal MERCURY. They used this symbolic presentation partly because of the religious intolerance which made it unsafe to promulgate any other teaching than that sanctioned by the orthodox church of that day, and partly because humanity as a whole was not yet ready to accept the truths which were embodied in their philosophy. They also spoke of a fourth element, AZOTH, a name composed of the first and last letters of our classical languages and intended to convey the same idea as "alpha and omega"--that of all-inclusiveness. This referred to what we now know as the spiritual ray of Neptune, which is the octave of Mercury and which is the sublimated essence of spiritual power.

The alchemists knew that the moral and physical nature of man had become gross and coarse on account of the passions inculcated by the Lucifer Spirits, and that, therefore, a process of distillation and refinement was necessary to eliminate these characteristics and elevate man to the sublime heights where the splendor of the spirit is no longer obscured by the coarse coating which now hides it from view. They therefore regarded the body as a laboratory and spoke of the spiritual processes in chemical terms. They noted that these processes have their inception and their particular field of activity in the spinal cord that forms the link between the two creative organs, THE BRAIN, which is the field of operation for the intellectual Mercurians, and THE GENITALS, which are the vantage ground of the sensuous and passionate Lucifer Spirits.

This tripartite spinal cord was to the alchemists the crucible of consciousness; they knew that in the sympathetic section of the cord which governs the functions that have to do particularly with the upkeep and welfare of the body, the Lunar Angels were specially active and this segment was therefore designated as the element SALT. The segment governing the motor nerves which expend the dynamic energy stored in the body by our food they saw clearly to be under the dominance of the Martial Lucifer Spirits, and they, therefore, named that segment SULPHUR. The remaining segment, which marks and registers the sensations carried by the nerves, was named MERCURY, because it was said to be under the dominance of spiritual beings from Mercury. THE SPINAL CANAL, contrary to the ideas of anatomists, is NOT filled with fluid, but with a gas that is like steam in that it may be condensed when exposed to the outside atmosphere, but may also be super- heated by the vibratory activity of the spirit to such an extent that it becomes a brilliant and luminous fire, the fire of purification and regeneration. This is the field of action of the great spiritual Hierarchy from Neptune and is designated AZOTH by the alchemists. This spiritual fire is not alike in every man nor is it as luminous in one as in another. The state thereof depends upon the spiritual advancement of the person in question.

When the aspirant to the higher life had been instructed in these mysteries of symbolism and the time had come to speak to him plainly, the following teachings were communicated to him, not necessarily in these words nor in this manner. But at any rate he was given to understand and it was made clear to him that--"anatomically man belongs to the animals, and that below that kingdom in the scale of evolution are the plants. They are pure and INNOCENT, their propagative practices are untainted by passion, and their WHOLE creative force is turned UPWARDS toward the light, where it manifests as the flower, a thing of joy and beauty for all to behold. Yet the plants are unable to do otherwise, for they have no intelligence, no consciousness of the outside world and no free-will in action. They can only create in the physical world, however.

"Above man in the scale of evolution are the gods, creators upon the spiritual and physical planes. They also are pure as the plants, for their WHOLE creative force is also turned UPWARDS and is expended in whatever manner their intelligence directs; and knowing good and evil, they always do good by choice.

"Between the gods and the plant kingdom stands man, a being endowed with intelligence, creative power and free-will to use it for good or ill. At present, however, he is dominated by the passion instilled by the Lucifer Spirits and sends one-half of his creative force DOWNWARD from the light to gratify his senses. In his innermost soul he realizes that this is wrong, and hence he hides his creative instinct in shame and is outraged when it is dragged into the light. This condition must be altered ere spiritual progress can be made, and, therefore, you must carefully consider the similarity between the chaste plant and the pure spiritual gods who BOTH TURN THEIR WHOLE CREATIVE POWER UPWARDS TOWARDS THE LIGHT. In the course of evolution you have risen above the plant, which has creative power only in the physical world, and have become like the gods possessing creative power, on both the mental and the physical planes of being, besides intelligence and free-will to direct it. This was accomplished by the diversion of one-half of your sex-force UPWARDS for building a brain and larynx, organs which are still fed and nourished by this uplifting half of the sexforce. But while the gods direct their WHOLE creative force to ALTRUISTIC PURPOSES by the power of mind, you still squander one-half of your divine heritage upon desire and sensegratification. If, therefore, you would become as they, YOU MUST LEARN TO TURN YOUR WHOLE CREATIVE ENERGY UPWARD TO BE USED UNDER THE DIRECTION OF YOUR INTELLIGENCE ENTIRELY. Thus only can you become as the gods and create from yourself by the power of your mind and the GREAT WORD whereby you may speak the creative fiat. Remember that PHYSICALLY you were once hermaphrodite like the plant and able to create from yourself. Look into the future now through the perspective of the past and realize that your present uni-sexual condition is only a temporary phase of evolution and that in the future your WHOLE creative force must be turned UPWARDS SO THAT YOU SHALL BECOME A HERMAPHRODITE SPIRITUALLY, and thus able to objectify your ideas and speak THE LIVING WORD which shall endue them with life and make them vibrant with vital energy. This DUAL creative force thus expressed through the brain and larynx is the 'ELIXIR-VITAE' which springs from THE LIVING STONE of the spiritually hermaphrodite philosopher. The alchemical process of kindling and elevating it is accomplished in the spinal cord where the SALT, SULPHUR, MERCURY and AZOTH are found. It is raised to incandescence by high and noble thought, by meditation upon spiritual subjects, and by altruism expressed in the daily life. The second half of the creative energy thus drawn upward through the spinal canal is a SPINAL SPIRIT-FIRE, the serpent of wisdom. Gradually it is raised higher and higher and when it reaches the pituitary body and the pineal gland in the brain, it sets them to vibrating, opening up the spiritual worlds and enabling man to commune with the gods. Then this fire radiates in all directions and permeates the whole body and its auric atmosphere, and man has become a LIVING STONE, whose luster surpasses that of the diamond or the ruby. HE IS THEN THE PHILOSOPHER'S STONE."

There are many other symbols and similes taken from the world of chemistry and applied to the processes of spiritual growth which eventually makes men living stones in the temple of God. But enough has been said in the foregoing to show what was meant by the ancient alchemists by such terms and the reason why they clothed their teachings in symbolical language. The way of initiation is, however, and has always bee open to anyone who really an truly seeks for enlightenment and is willing to pay the price in the coin of self-denial and selfsacrifice. Therefore, seek the temple door and you shall find it; knock and it shall be opened unto you. If you SEEK prayerfully, if you KNOCK persistently and if you LABOR manfully you will in time reach the goal and you will BECOME The Philosopher's Stone.

CELIBACY AND MARRIAGE

In order to avoid misunderstanding, it should be said that this lesson was only given to the aspirant to discipleship to show him the reason why it is necessary for him to live a pure and chaste life. It does not apply to the masses who have no spiritual aspirations and are as yet unable to restrain their passions. The Rosicrucians do not even advocate an entirely celibate life for their pupils; indeed they regard it as a religious duty for the enlightened mystic, man or woman, to wed a kindred spirit if such can be found, and thus furnish incoming souls a particularly advantageous opportunity for rebirth. When such a devoted couple perform the generative act in a spirit of aspiration to serve a waiting ego, when the prenatal conditions are pure mentally, morally and physically, when the early childhood days of the ego thus born are spent in a home atmosphere of high and noble thought, both parents and children are making wonderful progress. And as great souls cannot be born to ignoble parents any more than water can sink below its level, it would, indeed, be very wrong for aspirants to discipleship to live an entirely celibate life for the sake of self- advancement when conditions permit them to wed; furthermore, the expenditure of the creative force at the few times in a life when it is LEGITIMATELY REQUIRED for propagation would not seriously interfere with the spiritual development undertaken to BECOME The Philosopher's Stone, and the soul-growth gained by assuming the duties of parenthood would far outweigh any possible loss.

What the Rosicrucians teach then is that marriage between people who will limit their use of the creative function to the purpose of propagation is eminently good, noble and productive of great soul-growth, but that unmarried aspirant should live an absolutely celibate life if they wish to attain the highest.

PART VIII
THE PATH OF INITIATION

In an earlier chapter we noted that the transition of the Adept from the dominion of death to the realm of immortality was foreshadowed in the daring leap of Hiram Abiff, the Grand Master-Workman of Solomon's Temple, into the seething sea of molten metal and his passage through the nine arch-like strata of the earth which form the path of Initiation. We also remember that at the end of that journey Hiram Abiff, the son of Cain, received from his ancestor A NEW HAMMER AND A NEW WORD for use in the New Age. According to the Gospels we also find that Jesus, the son of Seth, immediately after his descent from Golgotha entered the subterranean strata where he remained for some time in communion with the spirits who dwell there. Thus the various strata of the earth from the circumference to the center form the path of Initiation, both for the sons of Seth and the sons of Cain, and that is the reason why little or nothing is said of the inner construction of the earth in the multitude of books dealing with subjects of occultism. Those who are simply psychics do not know, and those who do know are not saying much. There is a chapter on the subject in the Rosicrucian Cosmo-Conception which gives about all that one dares to tell, and to that the reader is referred for further information than here given.

The path of Initiation is guarded in various ways. While we walk the earth in our physical bodies, we are drawn toward the center of the earth by the force of gravitation; but our bodies being solid, that is to say, of the same density as the material whereof our globe is composed, we are thus prevented from sinking through the earth by displacement as we would sink in water, or by interpenetration as we would pass through ether. When death comes and we shed this so-called mortal coil, we find ourselves in vehicles that are finer than the elements of the earth. A person clothed in these finer vehicles could easily penetrate through the various strata of our globe to the center if there were no other obstacles. Having shed the dense body, he is no longer subject to gravitation, but to levitation, and on that account he usually finds it sufficiently difficult to stay upon the surface of the earth. Only during the first part of his post-mortem experience when he is still loaded down with the coarsest ether and desire stuff is this possible for him. The more he has gathered of that denser substance by indulgence of his lower nature and cultivation of the habit of drunkenness, covetousness, hatred, malice, immoral emotions, and disreputable vices, the easier it is for him to stay around low saloons, gambling houses, red-light districts, and kindred places. But the man of high ideals and lofty aspirations, who would be the one likely to seek the path of Initiation, feels the impelling force of levitation drawing him outward into the purer strata of the air where the First Heaven is located, and is thus effectually prevented from trespassing upon the path of Initiation. Stories are told of Initiates having overcome the law of gravitation in order to RISE IN THE AIR at certain times for a definite purpose while still in the dense body. Initiates are also taught how to suspend the law of levitation when they are in their soul bodies, and how to pass through the nine strata of the earth. It is said that Jesus was the son of a carpenter, but the Greek word is TEKTON, and means builder; ARCHE is the Greek name of primordial matter. It is also said that Jesus was a carpenter (tekton) himself. It is true, he was A TEKTON, builder or Mason, a Son of God, the Grand ARCHETEKTON. At the age of THIRTY-THREE, when he had taken the three-times-three (9) degrees of Mystic Masonry, he descended to the center of the earth. So does every other TEKTON, Mason or PHREE MESSEN, (CHILD OF LIGHT,) as the Egyptian called such, descend through the NINE arch-like strata of the earth. We shall find at the time of the first advent of Christ both Hiram Abiff, the son of Cain, and Solomon, the son of Seth, reborn to take from Him the next great Initiation into the Christian Mysteries.

In the last chapter we saw while considering "The Philosopher's Stone" that the spinal cord is the principal laboratory for the alchemist, and that the SPINAL SPIRIT FIRE, generated by turning the creative force upward through the spinal canal, passing it between the pituitary body and the pineal gland in the brain, gives to man a third eye as it were wherewith to see in the spiritual worlds. When this serpentine spirit fire has been sufficiently evolved, he may read by its light the wisdom of the ages. Therefore Christ exhorted His Disciples to be wise as serpents. The Egyptian word NAJA, which means serpent, is used at least once in the Hebrew Bible in the 58th Psalm. In ancient Egypt the Pharaohs were Kings and Priests, holding a double office, and they therefore wore a double crown with a URAEUS or serpent head so placed that when wearing this crown the URAEUS seemed to protrude from the Emperor's forehead between the eyebrows. The serpentine Uraeus was therefore an apt symbol of the wisdom of the wearer. It will be remembered that according to the Bible story the Lucifer Spirit appeared to Eve as a serpent, a son of Wisdom. Cain according to the Masonic legend, was born from this union with Eve. It is also stated that the Lucifer spirit then left Eve, who thus became a widow, and Cain was thus the son of the Lucifer Spirit, the serpent of Wisdom, and Eve, the widow. Every Initiate to this day has the serpent symbol on his brow and is known to his fellows by that token as a SON OF THE WIDOW AND THE LUCIFER SPIRIT. Therefore we shall trace Hiram Abiff to his next embodiment by that mark, and as evidence given by a party against his own interest is particularly valuable according to law, we call special attention to the following points gained from the Catholic Latin Testament: In 1st Samuel 19, King James Version, NAIOTH is spoken of as a place where a school of prophets and seers dwelt, Samuel among others. NAIOTH is the feminine plural of NAJA, a serpent, which we have already mentioned as being an Egyptian word used in the Bible. In the Latin version the same place is spoken of as NAIM, and Eusebius says it was located near Endor, famous as the abode of the witch, through whose instrumentality Saul spoke with Samuel after the latter had passed on. But it is not to be supposed that NAIOTH and NAIM are places, or that they were used interchangeably. They describe two widely different classes of spiritually gifted people, which the ancient Egyptians had marked by placing the URAEUS upon the BROWS of one and at the NAVELS of the other. The latter were mediumistic persons, receiving impressions from spirit controls through the solar plexus. They were properly designated Naioth by the Hebrews who used the feminine suffix to indicate their negative qualities. But the voluntary clairvoyant and the Initiate, represented by the Egyptians as having the serpentine URAEUS in the forehead, were called NAIM by the Hebrews who used the male suffix to designate the positive spiritual faculty which they possess. And the Latin Catholic version of the New Testament (Luke, vii, 11-15,) speaks of the person raised by Christ as the widow's son of NAIN.

As the serpent is not fully unfolded until the ninth arch of the Lesser Mysteries has been passed and the candidates become aspirants to the Greater Mysteries, and further because the Lodge of PHREE MESSEN (Children of Light) of Ancient Egypt are now transferred to the various branches of the Anglo-Saxon race, where the sound NAIN means "nine," the original word has been corrupted to mislead all not entitled to the knowledge. But all things change on this terrestrial sphere, and this applies also to the methods of Initiation and the requirements thereof. Hiram Abiff failed in his great effort to make the molten sea at the time when he was building Solomon's Temple, because he, the son of the fiery Lucifer Spirits, did not know how to blend the element fire with the water poured into his mold by the sons of Seth, the creatures of the water God, Jehovah. At that time he was given A NEW HAMMER AND A NEW WORD. The Hammer was in the form of a CROSS. The Word was written upon a DISC, before he was finally slain by his adversaries. And so he slept until as LAZARUS, THE WIDOW'S SON OF NAIN, he was raised by THE STRONG GRIP OF THE LION'S PAW, the Lion of Judah. Then the disc was found, also the new cruciform Hammer, and upon the disc the mystic symbol, THE ROSE. In these two symbols lie hidden the great secret of life, the blending of water and fire, as symbolized by the earthborn fluidic sap ascending through the stem and calyx of the flower to the fire tinted petals, born in the purity of the Sun, but still guarded by the thorns of the martial Lucifer spirits. Exoteric MASONRY, which is only the husks of the Mystic Order formed by the Sons of Cain, has in modern times attracted the MASCULINE element with its positively polarized physical vehicles, and educated them in industry and STATECRAFT, thus controlling the material development of the world. The sons of Seth, constituting themselves the Priestcraft, have worked their spell over the positive vital bodies of the FEMININE element of dominate spiritual development. And whereas, the sons of Cain working through Freemasonry and kindred movements, have openly fought for the temporal power, the Priestcraft has fought as strenuously and perhaps more effectively by stealth to retain their hold upon the spiritual development of the feminine element.

To the casual onlooker it would seem as if there were no decided antagonism between these two movements at the present time; but though Freemasonry of today is but a shell of its true ancient mystic self, and though Catholicism has been terribly tarnished by the touch of time, in this one thing there is no difference, namely, that the war is as keen as ever. The efforts of the Church are not concentrated upon the masses, however, as much as upon those who are seeking to live the higher life so that they may gain admission to the Mystery Temple and learn how to make the Philosopher's Stone. As mankind advances in evolution, the vital body becomes more permanently positively polarized, giving to both sexes a greater desire for spirituality, and though we change from the masculine to feminine in alternate embodiments, positive polarity of the vital body is becoming more pronounced regardless of sex. This accounts for the growing tendency towards Altruism which is even being brought out by the suffering entailed by the great war we are now fighting (1918), for all agree that the nations are seeking to obtain a LASTING PEACE where the swords may be made into plowshares, and the spears into pruning hooks. In the past, humanity has been claiming universal brotherhood as a great ideal, but we must come closer than that to being in full accord with the Christ. He said to His disciples "YE ARE MY FRIENDS." Among brothers and sisters, hate and enmity may exist, but friendship is the expression of love and cannot exist apart from that. Universal Friendship is therefore the magic word which will eventually level all distinctions, bring peace upon earth and good will among men. This is the great Ideal which points the shortest way to the New Heaven and the New Earth, where the sons of Cain and the sons of Seth will eventually be united.

PART IX
ARMAGEDDON, THE GREAT WAR, AND THE COMING AGE

The chart printed in Part V shows that there was an Age when humanity lived in peace and happiness under the guardianship of a ruler who held the DOUBLE OFFICE of King and Priest, being both temporal and spiritual head of the DOUBLE SEXED human race. He is called Melchisedec in the Bible terminology, and it is said that he was King of Salem, Salem meaning Peace. Since then humanity has been divided into TWO sexes, male and female, and placed under the dual rulership of a King having dominion over their temporal affairs and aiming to advance them by industry and STATECRAFT, and a Priest, head of the priestcraft, exercising a SPIRITUAL AUTHORITY, in such a manner as they considered for the ETERNAL good of their charges.

The statecraft employed by the sons of Cain holds up the MALE ideal, HIRAM ABIFF, the Master craftsman, the Son of FIRE, while the sons of Seth as priestcraft uphold the FEMALE ideal in the VIRGIN MARY, the lady of the sea.

Thus fire and water, male and female, Church and State, are opposed to each other, with the inevitable result that a great war has been waged ever since the separation, that sin, sorrow and death are rampant, and that humanity is praying for the day of redemption, when the two streams shall be united in the Kingdom of Heaven where there is NEITHER MARRYING NOR GIVING IN MARRIAGE, and where reigns Christ, the King of Peace, exercising the DUAL office of King and Priest after the order of Melchisedec, for the good of all.

But this new order can not come into existence in a day. It requires ages of preparation, not only of the land itself, but of the people who are to inhabit it. And in order to gain an idea of what that land is like, and how the people are constituted, it will be helpful to consider the evolutionary career of humanity which has brought us the land where we live to our present status; that will then give us the perspective to see what is in store for us in the future.

The Biblical and occult traditions agree with science that there was a time when darkness brooded over the deep of space, where the material for the coming earth planet was being gathered together and set in motion by the Divine Hierarchs; that this stage was followed by a period of luminosity, when the dark cloud of matter had become a fire mist; that this was followed by a period when the cold of space and the heat of the planet-in- the-making generated an atmosphere of steam close to the fiery core and mist further from the fiery center. When the mist had cooled sufficiently, it fell again as rain upon the fiery core, to be reevaporated, and this continued in endless cycles, until by repeated boiling of the waters, an incrustation began to form around the fiery core. Upon the islands of crust in the ocean of fire we first learn of humanity dwelling in solid physical bodies, where of course very dissimilar to those we have today. During the next stage the crust of the earth became sufficiently strong to cover the whole inner core, and humanity lived then in the basins of the earth, in the land of mist, which was so dense that breathing was accomplished by means of gill clefts similar to those of the fishes and still seen in human embryo.

When the mists of Atlantis commenced to settle, some of our forbears had grown embryonic lungs and were forced to the highlands years before their compeers. Therefore they wandered in the wilderness while the promised land as we know it today was emerging from the lighter fogs, and at the same time their growing lungs were fitting them to live under the present atmospheric conditions. Two more races were born in the basins of the earth after the pioneers had left it. Then a succession of floods drove them all to the highlands. The last flood took place when the Sun by precession entered the watery sign Cancer about ten thousand years ago, as told Plato by the Egyptian Priests. Thus we see that there is no sudden change of constitution or environment for the whole human race when a new epoch is ushered in, but an overlapping of conditions which makes it possible for the majority by gradual adjustment to enter the new conditions, though the change may seem sudden to the individual when the preparatory work has been accomplished unconsciously. The metamorphosis of a frog from a denizen of the water to the airy element give an analogy of the past emergence of humanity from the continent of Atlantis to the Rainbow Age of Aryana. And the transformation of an earth worm to a butterfly soaring the skies is an apt illustration of the coming change from our present state and condition to those of the New Galilee where the Kingdom of Christ will be established; and what the change in the human constitution and environment is to be, may be seen by examining the past conditions as outlined in the Bible, which agrees with the occult traditions in the main points. This New Heaven and New Earth is now in the making. When the heavenly time marker, the Sun, came into Aries by precession, a new cycle commenced and the glad tidings were preached by Christ. He said by implication that the New Heaven and Earth were not ready then, when He told his disciples "whither I go, you cannot NOW follow, but you shall follow afterwards; I go to prepare a place for you and will come again and receive you." Later, John saw in a vision the New Jerusalem descending from Heaven, and Paul taught the Thessalonians BY THE WORD OF THE LORD that those who are Christ's at His coming shall be caught up IN THE AIR to meet Him and be with Him for the Age. This is in line with the tendencies shown by past developments. The Lemurians lived very close to the fiery core of the earth. The Atlanteans inhabited the basins somewhat further away from the center. The Aryans were driven by the flood to the hilltops where they are now living. And analogously, the citizens of the coming Age will inhabit the air.

But we know that our dense body gravitates towards the center of the earth, therefore, a change must take place; also Paul tells us that flesh and blood cannot inherit the Kingdom of Heaven. But he also points out that we have a SOMA PSUCHICON (mistranslated natural body,) a SOUL BODY, and this is made of ether, which is lighter than air and therefore capable of levitation. This is the Golden Wedding Garment, the Philosopher's Stone, or the Living Stone, spoken of in some of the ancient philosophies as the Diamond Soul, for it is luminous, lustrous, and sparkling--a priceless gem. It was also called the ASTRAL BODY by the Mediaeval Alchemists, because of the ability it conferred upon the one who has it to traverse the starry regions. But it is not to be confounded with the Desire Body which some of the modern pseudo-occultists mistakenly call the Astral Body. This vehicle, the Soul Body, will eventually be evolved by humanity as a whole, but during the change from the Aryan epoch to the ethereal conditions of the New Galilee, there will be pioneers who precede their brethren as the original Semites did in the change from Atlantis to Aryana. Christ mentioned this class in Matthew, 11th chapter, 12th verse, when He said: "The Kingdom of Heaven suffereth violence, and the violent take it by force." That is not a correct translation. It ought to be "The Kingdom of the Heavens has been invaded" (the Greek is biaxetai,) "and invaders seize on her." Men and women already have learned through a holy, helpful life to lay aside the body of flesh and blood, either intermittently or permanently, and to walk the skies with winged feet, intent upon the business of their Lord, clad in the ethereal wedding garment of the new dispensation.

This change may have been accomplished through a life of simple helpfulness and prayer as practiced by devoted Christians, no matter with what church they are affiliated if they follow the path of the Sons of Seth. Others have attained by following the specific exercises given by the Rosicrucians.

And thus the process of the unification of the two streams is already under way. But the war between the flesh and the spirit is still raging in the breast of most people as fiercely as it was in the days when Paul gave vent to his pent up feelings, and told us how the flesh was warring against the spirit within himself, and how he did the wrong things which he would not do, and omitted good deed which he aspired so ardently to perform. Nor will the struggle ever cease for the Mystic Mason until he has learned to build the Temple made without hands, which is not completed until he has come to the Eighteenth (1 plus 8) Degree, which is the Degree of the Rose Croix.

This is the ultimate of the Thirty-third Degree, for three times three are nine, and one plus eight are nine. Nine being the highest degree in the Lesser Mysteries, he who has passed this degree of the genuine Mystic Order is then, and then only, the WIDOW'S SON OF NINE, or NAIN, ready to be raised by the strong grip of the paw of the Lion of Judah, to the Kingdom of the Heavens, there to receive the "well done, thou good and faithful servant, enter into the joy of your Lord" for "Him that overcometh will I make A PILLAR in the House of God, thence he shall no more go out." He is then immortal, loosed from the wheel of Birth and Death.

SUMMARY

In conclusion, it may be well to sum up the points which have been made in these articles on Freemasonry and Catholicism, it being understood that the term "Catholicism" as here used does not refer to the Roman Catholic Church alone, "Catholic" being taken in the sense of UNIVERSAL, so that the term includes all movements inaugurated by the Sons of Seth, the Priestcraft.

The origin of the temporal and spiritual streams of evolution is as follows: Jehovah created Eve, a human being.

The Lucifer Spirit Samael united with Eve and begat a semi-divine son, Cain. As he left Eve before the birth of the child, CAIN WAS THE SON OF A WIDOW, AND A SERPENT OF WISDOM.

Then Jehovah created Adam, a human being like Eve.

Adam and Eve united and begat a child, human like themselves, whose name was Abel. Jehovah, being the Lunar God, is associated with the water, hence there was enmity between CAIN, THE SON OF FIRE, and ABEL, THE SON OF WATER. So Cain slew Abel and Abel was replaced by Seth.

In time and through generations, the Sons of Cain became the CRAFTSMEN of the world, skilled in the use of fire and metal. Their ideal was MALE, Hiram Abiff, the Master workman.

The Sons of Seth, on the other hand, became the CHURCHMEN, upholding the FEMININE ideal, the Virgin Mary, and ruling their people by the magic WATER placed at their temple doors.

Various attempts have been made to unite the two streams of humanity and emancipate them from their progenitors, Jehovah and the Lucifer Spirits.

With this end in view the symbolical TEMPLE was built according to the instruction of SOLOMON, the Son of Seth and the Molten Sea was cast by HIRAM ABIFF, the Son of Cain; but the main object was frustrated as we have seen, and the attempt at unification proved abortive.

Moses, the divinely appointed leader of the old dispensation, afterward reborn as Elijah, guided humanity through its ages of infancy, and was finally embodied as John the Baptist, the herald of the new dispensation, the Christian Era. At the same point in time the other actors in the World Drama were also brought to birth that they might serve their brothers.

At the casting of the Molten Sea HIRAM ABIFF had been given the baptism of fire by Cain, which freed him from the LUCIFER SPIRITS; he was also given a new Hammer and a new Word. When the new Era dawned, he was born as Lazarus, the widow's son of Nain, and raised by the strong grip of the lion's paw to the rank of Immortals as Christian Rosenkreuz.

SOLOMON, the Son of Seth, was reborn as JESUS. The BAPTISM OF WATER administered by John as representative of Jehovah freed him also. He yielded his body at that moment to the descending Christ Spirit and ranged himself with the new leader.

Religion has been terribly tarnished in the course of time, its pristine purity has long since vanished under the regime of creed, and it is no longer CATHOLIC, that is to say, UNIVERSAL. Sects and "isms" have branched out in one direction and another, but still JESUS from the invisible worlds enfolds in his love all THE SONS OF SETH who will call upon his name BY FAITH, and he will eventually unite the scattered churches in the Kingdom of Christ.

CHRISTIAN ROSENKREUZ was given charge of the Sons of Cain who seek the light of KNOWLEDGE at the sacred fires of the Mystic Shrine. As the creative energy implanted by their divine ancestor Samael caused Cain to work out their own salvation through the fire of tribulation, and fashion for themselves the Golden Wedding Garment, which is the "Open Sesame" to the

Invisible World. And though the cleansing blood of Jesus is an absolute necessity to millions of weaker brothers, there can scarcely be any question when we assert that THE MORE MEN AND WOMEN WHO ENGAGE IN MYSTIC MASONRY TO CONSCIOUSLY BUILD THIS TEMPLE OF THE SOUL, THE SOONER WE SHALL SEE THE SECOND ADVENT OF CHRIST, AND THE STRONGER WILL BE THE RACE WHICH HE SHALL RULE BY THE LAW OF LOVE.

www.ingramcontent.com/pod-product-compliance
Lightning Source LLC
LaVergne TN
LVHW041635070426
835507LV00008B/643